# YOU'RE PROBABLY NOT CRAZY

A Book For Emotional Women,
Written By An Emotional Woman

**JANINE JEANSON**

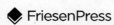 FriesenPress

Suite 300 - 990 Fort St
Victoria, BC, V8V 3K2
Canada

www.friesenpress.com

**Copyright © 2021 by Janine Jeanson**
First Edition — 2021

All rights reserved.

No part of this publication may be reproduced in any form, or by any means, electronic or mechanical, including photocopying, recording, or any information browsing, storage, or retrieval system, without permission in writing from FriesenPress.

ISBN
978-1-03-910538-6 (Hardcover)
978-1-03-910537-9 (Paperback)
978-1-03-910539-3 (eBook)

1. SELF-HELP, EMOTIONS

Distributed to the trade by The Ingram Book Company

*For Joanne, who always listened.*

# TABLE OF CONTENTS

Chapter 1: Epiphanies — 1
Chapter 2: The Stereotypes — 7
Chapter 3: Lies — 15
Chapter 4: Repression — 23
Chapter 5: Discomfort — 31
Chapter 6: The Tough Questions — 39
Chapter 7: Nasty Woman: Women in Politics — 45
Chapter 8: 45's Meltdown — 57
Chapter 9: Women in Media — 63
Chapter 10: How Underestimating Women Limits Society — 73
Chapter 11: Women, Emotions & Relationships — 81
Chapter 12: Let Toxicity Go — 89
Chapter 13: Women Supporting Women — 95
Chapter 14: Ignore Others & Listen To You — 103
Chapter 15: The Angry Woman — 109
Chapter 16: Fear Conqueror — 117
Chapter 17: Feeling the Pressure — 123
Chapter 18: Superstar — 131
Chapter 19: No — 137

Chapter 20: What Are We Afraid Of?                    143
Chapter 21: Men & Their Emotions                      151
Chapter 22: My Bachelor-Watching Origin Story         161
Chapter 23: The Double Standards                      165
Chapter 24: Men Leading By Example                    173
Chapter 25: The Importance of Emotional Education     181
Chapter 26: Little Emotions                           189
Chapter 27: On Being a Drama Queen                    195
Chapter 28: Say Goodbye to Proper                     201
Chapter 29: Owning Your Emotions                      205
Chapter 30: What I've Learned                         211
Chapter 31: Yes Babe, Feel!                           219
About the Author

# 1
# Epiphanies

*"Well behaved women seldom make history"*
*– Laurel Thatcher Ulrich*

I was talking with my mom a little while back, and we somehow got on the subject of women and their treatment in society. As usual, I got onto a big rant about how unfairly we are treated in this world. We were talking about how women are thought of as overly emotional when I said to my mom, half jokingly, "You know, I'd rather deal with an emotional woman than deal with an emotional man."

At this point I was getting pretty passionate about it. Then my mom said, "You should write a book. You have a lot of feelings."

I laughed it off with a sarcastic, "Okay Mom," but the more I thought about it, the more appealing the idea of writing a book sounded. Hearing her tell me I had a lot of feelings got me thinking about feelings in general.

In that moment I started to really process all the injustices, inequality, body-shaming, pressure, stereotypes, and so much more bullshit women have to deal with every day. It started to make me really angry. Like really fucking angry. Even though I've been living with all of this my whole life, it was like my eyes were opened to it for the first time. These ideas and these feelings hit me really hard, very suddenly. I decided I needed to do something about it.

I was really excited, because I never thought I would write a book about the opinions and feelings I have. I got really into it and would write for hours a day, calling my parents after I finished every chapter. But then I started to get a little discouraged. I thought to myself, "Who's ever going to read this book? What am I doing this for?"

The more I thought about it, the more I realized I'm doing this for me, and if someone else reads it along the way, even better. It doesn't matter to me if anyone reads this book. This is what I needed to do in order to feel like I was making a difference. For that, I'm pretty proud.

Another reason I wrote this book is because there are so many good men out there who might not realize what women go through on a daily basis. I thought if I could provide them with some insight it might lead them to advocate for change. How can we expect men to make changes if they're unaware changes need to be made?

I've always had a lot of feelings and emotions. And thinking of all of this made me realize how much people, but especially women, are punished for having these feelings. It's something that's really held us back, through no fault of our own, but through a society that has us conditioned to believe negative things about the way women show emotions. I've spent my whole life trying to be polite and kind to other people because that's what we're supposed to do.

I used to take acting classes, and I was working on a scene when my teacher told me, "You're being too polite to your partner." She told me to stop being so nice to him because I wasn't doing either of us any favours by being this way. The scene was boring. I was letting him win the scene. Emotions add colour in acting, just like they do in real life. I have been so conditioned to be polite and kind, especially to men, and this acting class highlighted how willing I was to give them the easy way out. This is the way I am in real life.

As I thought, I questioned how many times I had let men win in the past. The answer is, a lot, and I really hate that it is. It makes me so angry to think about all the times I let a man win when they didn't deserve it. It's who I am as a person though. I'm not aggressive or challenging because I've been made to believe good girls don't behave this way. All women are made to believe some variation of this, and it has done nothing but hurt us.

A long time ago, some people decided they didn't like the way women showed emotions. And their misogynistic asses also decided the worst thing in the world for men was to be seen as womanly. So that was it. Bam! No more emotions allowed.

All women are victims of stereotypes. We live in a world that expects so much of girls, but gives them so little in return. We've been told our whole lives how we should act in every situation. I'm done adhering to a set of rules aimed at bringing women down. I'm also tired of listening to stories of women being treated badly just for being women.

I'm tired, plain and simple. Women deserve so much more than what society is giving to them. They have always deserved more. For the women who are reading this book, I hope you're tired too.

You should be.

# 2

# The Stereotypes

*"Girls are capable of doing everything men are capable of doing. Sometimes they have more imagination than men."*

– *Katherine Johnson*

Women have heard countless times they are unfit to do something because they are "too emotional." The first time I heard it I was just a little girl, and while I don't remember why it was said to me, those words always stuck. Because of this, I have grown up trying not to cry in front of certain people, or show too much emotion for fear of being labelled as weak, or "unfit." I have thought about this a lot because I am an emotional person who has been known to cry every once in a while (or a lot). I also know people have judged me for it, and I have been told to stop crying or stop being so emotional. So I grew up repressing my sadness, and walked around like I wasn't about to break out in tears at any second. For anyone who has experienced this, you know what an awful feeling it is.

I don't know a single woman who hasn't heard they are unfit to do something because of their emotions. Or who hasn't tried to hide their emotions because they don't want to be judged simply for having them. If you are a woman reading this book, I want you to ask yourself right now if you've heard those words, or a variation of them. I would also like you to ask yourself if there was ever a time in your life you tried to hide the way you were feeling because you thought showing emotions might come back to hurt you in some way. I can guarantee you your answer is "yes."

Women are stereotyped as being emotional because they cry, or they care too much. We have come to associate the word "emotional" to mean crying, or sadness. But being emotional is so much more than just crying.

Men are known to show anger, or irritability, yet they are not seen as being emotional. How can anger, a very strong emotion, not be seen as emotional? It's because there are negative stereotypes associated with being a girl. Some men don't want to possess qualities typically viewed as female. So we've twisted the word and pigeonholed women as being the emotional ones, when in reality we all show our feelings. We just haven't learned to accept all emotions as valid.

However, even when a woman shows anger people will believe she's being crazy, largely because she is acting outside of the stereotypes individuals have set for her. I hate that women have been given the crazy label for showing their feelings. Anger does not make women crazy, but because society has said women have to be nurturing and kind, we can't handle when a woman gets angry. There are individuals that literally don't know what to do when faced with an angry woman. Acting in any way that's outside these ridiculous societal norms we've set for women can cause people to have negative perceptions of them.

When women become emotional, people assume that we MUST be on our periods. Why must we be menstruating in order for our emotions to be validated? Thankfully it's been a long time since someone seriously asked if I was on my period when I was being emotional, but it is commonly said to other women. We are constantly expected to be and act a certain way, so when we deviate from this behaviour people chalk it up to hormones, because it is too difficult to understand this might be normal behaviour. Women are allowed to be really angry or really sad without being on their period. To some it might sound like a crazy concept, but women are, in fact, human beings, and as human beings they are going to experience a wide range of emotions.

Showing feelings has taken its toll on women as a whole. Many women have been passed up for promotions or jobs, or have lost elected positions simply because people view them as being emotionally unfit to handle high pressure situations. Women who have never cried a day in their lives have been passed up for these positions on the basis that they might be prone to tears. Either way, it's often a lose/lose situation for women, whether they are criers or not. If a woman is emotional, she is seen as unfit. If a woman is not typically emotional there is the belief that she may become that way, so she is also seen as unfit. Lose freakin' lose.

People have said they don't trust women in important positions because their emotions might lead them to make harmful decisions. But men are just as likely to do this—they can make decisions based on their emotions, and make decisions when they are emotional without anyone questioning it. No one is saying that men are more in control of their emotions, they're saying men aren't emotional period. These are two very different things. Anger and passion are not seen as an overly emotional response, two emotions that are typically thought of as "manly". I would argue that those two responses are incredibly emotional. But we ignore that fact because of the way we view emotions, and the way we view men, versus the way we view women. People can't claim women make bad decisions based on their emotions, but then close their eyes to the decisions men make when they are angry or passionate. If we think being emotional makes you incapable of holding important positions we have to apply that to everyone, and not just women. No matter what the emotion is.

For those who argue that emotions should be kept out of decision making, I invite you to think about the actual possibility of removing feelings from the decision-making process. Of course there are feelings involved in decision making. Everything humans do is based, in some way, around emotions. It is important, however, that these feelings don't completely cloud one's judgment when making decisions. Men and women are equally capable of doing this!

The stereotypes, unfortunately, don't end here. We've all heard boys laugh and say to their friends "you _____ like a girl," like it's the worst insult possible. Men showing any sort of femininity would usually result in them being insulted or ridiculed. However, when women show masculine qualities, they are praised. The classic "oh she's into sports, who would have thought?" trope is very common. Why is it completely unbelievable that a girl could be good at, or interested in sports? Men love women who like sports; they think it's the sexiest thing in the world. If that's something that turns men on, all the power to them. I'm not here to judge anybody. But when men find out that another man is interested in something viewed as female, such as sewing or pottery, they are often made fun of. This is a really toxic way of thinking. It forces men to stay away from hobbies they want to pursue, and makes us believe the things women are interested in, like sewing, are trivial and unimportant.

I used to say "you _____ like a girl" all the time when I was young. Then I grew up and realized how stupid saying shit like that is. Once I realized how sexist it was, I simply stopped using it, and I would prefer that everyone stop using it as a derogatory phrase. And just so we're clear, wanting people to stop using this language doesn't make me overly sensitive. If you think the same way, you are not overly sensitive either. Sue us for wanting people to stop using our entire gender as a way to degrade the abilities of other people. It's insulting and it's damaging to women when they are the subject of negativity. The majority of people who say things like this aren't doing it to try and hurt people. It's been a common phrase that has been said for decades.

People still speak this way to me today, and when I hear it for a split second it makes me embarrassed about being a girl. It's fucked up, but that's the way I used to feel as a kid, except on a much larger scale. I used to hear it a lot more frequently when I was little, and I would always feel ashamed about not being able to do things as well as the boys. When I hear it today, it brings back all those feelings I had in my youth, and it drives me crazy. It goes to show how much something like that can stick with you, and how it can affect the way someone feels about themselves. I'm old enough to know better, and now I'm much more equipped to let stupid shit like that roll off my back. As a kid, though, I didn't understand sexism. To me, I was just not as capable of doing as many things as the boys were.

When we speak this way it portrays women as weak physically, mentally and emotionally. It implies we are weaker than men, and therefore not as capable of doing everything men are capable of.

These stereotypes have hurt women in many different ways. The language we use is more powerful than people realize. Whether it is meant maliciously or not, these words shape the way people think about women. We, to a degree, believe these things are true when we hear them, even if we know deep down they aren't. And when these words are delivered with a negative connotation we can't help but associate these stereotypes with negativity. We need to change the language we use, we need to be more careful with what we say, and we need to do better by women. It's especially important when speaking to children. Boys should know that men and women are equal, and that being a girl is awesome. And girls should believe that "run like a girl" means to run like the wind.

Every single woman I know has been negatively affected by these stereotypes in some way. Every woman is thought less of by some men because of the way we show our feelings. It's a constant battle to be seen as equal to our male counterparts, and thinking we're uncontrollably emotional has hurt us more than people seem to understand. It isn't just the stereotypes about our emotions that need to be addressed. An overall negative view of women makes some people view everything we do as annoying or unimportant. The attack on our emotions may seem like a small thing, but it has a big impact on the way people perceive women.

It's also unfair for society to deny men having certain interests. They should be allowed to enjoy whatever they want without being made fun of. It's probably a pretty shitty feeling when someone is made fun of for simply trying to enjoy their life. It's dumb as fuck if you really think about it. Why do we care so much about what other people do? Why do some people get so affected by the way other people want to live their lives? It must be so exhausting. Encouraging men to explore these typically more feminine interests will not only allow men to do whatever the fuck they want, but may teach them to explore their softer sides. It may also help them learn more about women, and be more understanding of women and our emotions and interests. Encouraging people to do the things they love will give them outlets for expressing their feelings. Men may find that something like baking allows them an emotional release, or a way to relieve stress. Who are we to deny them this? It's completely unfair. People are not one dimensional. It's insane to think that all men have to be interested in certain things, and can never like anything outside that box.

In order to accept our emotions as being valid, we need to break all stereotypes. We need to accept that women may sometimes feel things differently and are different than men. And we need to stop talking down about women and the things that are viewed as being "female." These qualities should not be seen as weak, but rather celebrated in both women and men. Women have so much to offer in this world, and it's time we recognize their contributions and capabilities—not just the ones society deems most acceptable.

# 3
# Lies

"For most of history Anonymous was a woman"
– *Virginia Wolfe*

*Women are soft.*
*Women are weak.*
*Women aren't fit.*
*Women aren't capable.*
*Women must have kids. It's their duty. It's the only way they'll be happy.*
*Women have to be thin.*
*Women have to look a certain way.*
*Women have to act a certain way.*
*Women are emotional.*
*Women are manipulative.*
*Women are crazy.*
*Women don't enjoy sex. They won't orgasm, so don't try to make it happen.*
*Women shouldn't make important decisions.*
*Women aren't good at math. Don't let them handle finances.*

Lies. All of them.

Women have been fed this story forever. We've been conditioned by society to believe these things about ourselves, and so we've gone through life not questioning any of it. We've been told we have our duties, and we must follow them.

Forget everything you've ever been taught. Question everything.

Women have often been made the villains of life's story. We talk about how unreasonable, crazy and emotional they are. How we shouldn't let them do certain things for fear of what might happen in their incapable hands. We've been told they'll lie and manipulate you and take away your freedom. Women are the old ball and chain. We even feel the need to make wedding cake toppers of women dragging men down the aisle because society needs to know men are now in prison, rather than a marriage. And women go along with it because it's hammered into them so much they don't even stop to think about how fucked up it all is. Women are not a burden, but society has us convinced we are, without most of us even realizing it. It's all bullshit.

Shit-talking a wedding cake topper may seem trivial, but it's part of a much larger issue of men being viewed as sane and women being crazy and out of control. I don't want to be thought of as a burden, or some crazy psychopath, and I don't appreciate that we say a man's life is over as soon as he commits to a marriage with a woman.

Some men enjoy being married, and like who they are married to. They should be able to express this without ridicule. They should be able to say "I like my wife and I like doing things with her" and not have to worry about what their friends will say about it. Even if it's all in good fun, ridiculing someone for this perpetuates the belief that marriage is a trap, and hanging out with your wife is a chore. Usually when women say "I'm hanging out with my husband" it isn't met with ridicule from other women.

I don't like these jokes. I know other women don't like these jokes. This doesn't mean that women don't have a sense of humour - something else women are often criticized for. These jokes have a time and a place. But when women constantly hear they are insufferable or difficult to live with, the jokes start to lose a little bit of their charm.

My dad loves golfing. In the summer he golfs every single day. Do you know who my dad's favourite person to golf with is? My mom. Not only does he enjoy spending time with my mom, and has no problem saying it, he loves doing a typically more "male activity" with her. In contrast there are some men who believe they should have women only golf courses. Have these men ever golfed with their wives or partners, and took a moment to appreciate the time they are spending together? I would say probably not. These men are led to believe they can't enjoy doing certain activities with their wives because of the lies society has continued to pump out about women.

Showing your emotions does not make you insane. Communicating your feelings isn't a bad thing, and it's not something you should try to hide. Sensitivity isn't a weakness, and I actually think it's beautiful how affected some people can get by the events taking place around them. If something hurts you, it hurts you. There's nothing you can do about your feelings, but I can tell you it doesn't mean you are any less capable of doing certain things.

We believe these lies because they are consistently thrown at us through every outlet possible. We see it and hear it in the media. We see it flashed on billboards. We see it at our own goddamn weddings. We hear it spoken in front of us and we don't bat an eye because we've accepted this is what we're like. This is the way we are seen. We have been conditioned to be comfortable with it. But I'm not comfortable with it. And neither should anyone else be.

Women have historically been seen as useful mainly because of our bodies. We bear children, and that's the most important thing about us. That's our most important function. Thank god we've been moving further and further away from this way of thinking, but women's bodies are still always up for discussion. And when we finally started taking control of our own bodies and celebrating them in the way we wanted to, we were shamed for it. Sometimes the words said about the ownership of our bodies can be brutal and painful. Breaking free from these preconceived notions is not easy. There will be challenges along the way, but once you do break free from it, I can assure you it's liberating as hell.

It's also important to live your life the way you want to. Never do something because you think it's what you should be doing. Don't fall into this trap society has set. If you don't want to have kids, then don't have kids. It isn't your duty to do so. They aren't going to fill this imaginary void we've been told about. I think most women have been told that kids will give our lives purpose, and when we get older our kids will make us less lonely. Don't have kids for this reason alone. There's no point in having them for a potentially less lonely future if it'll make your present more miserable. There are also several other things you can do to ensure your later years aren't lonely. The point is, don't do things because you think it's what you have to do. Live your life the way you want to, and don't believe the lies you've been hearing since the day you were born. It might take a little (or a lot) of self-reflection in order to find a way to be the happiest and best version of yourself.

I'm a victim of these lies. I have managed to alter my way of thinking about myself so that I no longer believe most of the horrible things people say about my gender. Although I no longer believe most of them, it doesn't change the fact that I'm insecure about myself. I sometimes find myself feeling ashamed of who I am and the way I act because it goes against what I've been taught. It's a constant battle to overcome these insecurities and little changes can go a long way in aiding women down a path of self-acceptance.

These lies were created to control women. If we believe to our core we are supposed to be a certain way, or can't do certain things, we'll never challenge it. For a long time, the vast majority of women didn't challenge it. Women were controlled by men. Men felt that it was their duty to control women. But women's stories are now being rewritten.

*Women are tough.*
*Women are strong.*
*Women are fit.*
*Women are capable.*
*Women don't need kids to be happy. They can want or not want them.*
*Women's bodies are different. They are all beautiful.*
*Women can look however they want.*
*Women can be who they are.*
*Women are emotional, and their emotions are valid.*
*Women aren't manipulative. Ignore the stereotypes.*
*Women aren't crazy. Ignore the stereotypes.*
*Women enjoy sex. Learn how to make them orgasm. Learn about women's bodies.*
*Women are capable of making important decisions.*
*Women are good at math.*
*Women can do anything they want to do.*
*Women can be anything they want to be.*

# 4
# Repression

*"I really think a champion is defined not by their wins but by how they can recover when they fall"*

*– Serena Williams*

Repression is something most people are familiar with. I believe we have all repressed the way we were feeling at some point in our lives, and I think we can all agree doing this is not helpful. I also think repression is something a lot of women do regularly. We don't feel like we can show our emotions to certain people, and so we just never show them.

My wonderful mother is an example of this. I am twenty-eight years old, and I have very rarely seen my mom upset. Yet, I know in my twenty-eight years of life there had to have been times where she felt incredible sadness. She always felt the need to be strong in front of my sister and me, and I think she didn't want to burden us with her problems. This is very typical of women. They put so many people before themselves, and they feel the need to stay strong for others. I love my mom for being the super strong and caring person she is, but I also would have loved for her to come to me when she was upset. Especially as I got older.

We have made some progress with her, despite her stubbornly telling us that everything is fine, even though it clearly isn't. Her positivity is something to be admired; I will never fault her for that. She always makes us feel like we can go to her for anything, and we have, but I have to wonder how it affected her. Or I wonder how many times she put our problems ahead of her own. It makes me sad to know that she could have been suffering and didn't come to me to address her feelings. If she was able to be emotionally vulnerable with me, I think it would show me a side of her I haven't seen before. No part of me would judge that side of her, or think any less of her for it. If anything, I would find it really great. I want her, and all women, to feel like they can be upset. That it's okay to turn it off every once in a while, and just feel your feelings.

I was watching the movie *I, Tonya* recently, and there was a scene in the movie that really stood out to me. If you've seen the movie, you'll know what I'm talking about. If you don't know what I'm talking about, I strongly suggest you take a look at this particular moment in the film.

Margot Robbie, the actor who plays Tonya Harding, is looking at herself in the mirror before a major performance, and she's pretty hysterical. She's been through some shit, and it's taking its toll on her, emotionally and mentally. She's looking in the mirror with tears running down her face, but she pulls herself together and puts on a fake, but passable, smile. She knows she has to perform, and she knows it's what she has to do. It was absolutely heartbreaking for me to watch. The scene stuck with me for two reasons. First, Margot Robbie is incredible, and she acted flawlessly. Secondly, it was relatable as hell. I have seen so many girls and women crying in the bathroom. They let it out for two minutes and then wipe their tears and slap a smile on their faces, because heaven forbid someone knows they've been crying. I've done it, my friends have done it, and I know we are not alone in doing this.

Doesn't it take so much courage and bravery to do something like this? Think about it. These women obviously have a lot going on in their lives, yet they are able to go about their day like nothing is wrong. They are at the point where they are crying in a bathroom or closet, but they pretend like everything's okay because people need them to be strong. And they are. The fact they are hiding their emotions doesn't mean they aren't emotional, it just means they've gotten pretty good at hiding their emotions. Everything they are feeling is there, and just because you can't see it doesn't mean it doesn't exist. We feel upset, but we walk around like nothing is wrong. We have big smiles on our faces, and we laugh like everything is fine, and we talk to people like everything is more than fine. That's because we feel like we have to do this. It's not enough to be neutral. We have to be happy.

A lot of expectations are placed on women to behave in a certain way. Expectations men don't have to deal with. So much of our value is placed on our physical appearance, and when we aren't happy on the outside people become uncomfortable. This is why some men tell us to smile more. They expect us to be good little girls who always have a smile plastered to their faces. We have created a society that expects us to look and behave a certain way. These expectations lead women to hide the way they're feeling. We repress our emotions and act in a way completely opposite to how we're feeling, all for the benefit of other people. But no one has stopped to think what this is doing to us inside. No one can be happy all the time, and there's nothing wrong with that. Repressing your feelings like this will only cause you harm. Stop doing things for the benefit of others, and start doing things that will make you the best version of yourself.

I've had men tell me to smile more walking down the street, and it's such a dumb thing for them to say. It makes me so much angrier than a typical catcall. First of all, we've been telling men for the longest time that "hey baby, you should smile more" is an unacceptable thing to say to a woman. Of course this doesn't apply to all men out there. I know men who would never even think about catcalling a woman, or telling someone to slap a smile on their face. The mere thought of it would make these men feel embarrassed. But there still is a large number of men who do these things. It's a persistent problem women face when walking down the street minding their own goddamn business. But some men don't care about how we feel about the catcalling because they don't take what we say seriously. It's also insane to tell someone you have no personal connection to how to feel. Nobody knows what other people are going through. What if the woman they're telling to smile just lost someone or something very important to them? It makes the man saying this look like a complete jackass. But again, they don't care what's going on in a woman's life. These men are only concerned about what they want and how they want a woman to look on the outside. Because that's more important than her feelings, right? Fuck off. No wonder women repress their emotions.

It makes me sad that women think they have to hide their feelings. There is a double standard in the way women have to hide their feelings, yet we allow men to get away with showing anger in public. This show of public anger is largely accepted, and the chance that men's reputations would be ruined for doing this is slim. You don't see men running into the bathroom to get angry. In fact, we normally don't even bat an eye when they do publicly show this type of behaviour. It is what it is. If a man were to get angry everyone would quickly forget about it and move on. The same wouldn't happen for a woman. If she were to cry in full view of everyone people would talk about it, and probably not in a nice way. To go a step further, if a woman were to get angry people would say she was being too emotional. Women aren't allowed to get angry because people will view them as bitchy and psycho. Either way, women can't win. If they cry, they're too emotional; if they get angry, they're still too emotional. When women show any sort of emotion at all, it's often met with judgement. None of it makes any sense. I just want to be able to show my damn feelings without someone reading so much into it. I'm not a robot, and I shouldn't have to act as such in order to be taken seriously in this world.

There have been countless times where I have wanted to cry, but I didn't. I tried so hard to keep it in for fear of looking stupid. To this day I still struggle with being vulnerable with people because I know it might lead to tears. I especially feel this with men. I find even now that when I'm talking to my male friends about something I'm upset about, I always give them a warning that they might see me cry. I usually don't end up crying though, because I alter my way of explaining the story because I'm scared to cry in front of them. With my close female friends, I couldn't care less if they see me cry. It bothers me that I do this. Why do I feel the need to hide the way I'm feeling because I'll cry? Looking back on it I wish that I had allowed myself to feel my feelings. Working on my vulnerability is always something I'm going to have to do, but it's my goal to stop repressing the way I'm feeling so much. Friends, male or female, should be there for you. If they judge you for crying, maybe they aren't such good friends after all.

I know my male friends wouldn't judge me for crying, but I am still incapable of doing it with the majority of them, and it bothers me. It's because I have grown up in a society that tells me men don't accept tears, and so in the back of my mind I think they won't accept them. I believe this way of thinking is unfair to my male friends. I understand it's a product of the society I grew up in, but it's also up to me to help change it. I need to start being more open with them if I'm ever going to expect to see some sort of change in this world. And although being more vulnerable with them is a scary thought, it would probably be helpful. It would help me be less scared of my emotions, and it would help men be more comfortable with crying women. Something I think we should all be more comfortable with.

Repressing feelings is usually not a good option for any of us. I've learned that talking to people about my feelings is important, and it's helped me through some difficult times. Having someone to listen to you is necessary. I know we all want to appear to be strong all the time, but have someone in your life who will just listen to you. Repressing your feelings will not cause them to go away. If anything, they will continue to build, which can eventually take its toll on you both mentally and physically.

## 5

# Discomfort

*"Do not wait for someone else to come and speak for you. It's you who can change the world."*

– Malala Yousefzai

People are uncomfortable with emotions. Have you ever been present when someone was getting yelled at, or when someone was hysterically crying? It doesn't necessarily have to involve you, but looking in on it is enough to make some people die of secondhand embarrassment. It's largely true when men, especially in positions of power, are dealing with emotional women.

I met up with my best friend one day and she was very upset. She had met with her male boss to discuss her performance at work and he had said some things that were hard for her to hear. She was also going through some things in her personal life and was finding it difficult to balance her work and home life. When he confronted her, she explained it was a difficult time for her, and immediately started to cry in front of him. He got very uncomfortable with her crying and didn't know how to respond to her. He also didn't provide very much comfort. As her boss he could have at least treated her like her feelings were important to him. They continued to discuss the issues and he explained that the reason why he was bringing her performance issues up was because when he hired her he had expected her to be a cheerleader for the office, and that recently she hadn't been living up to that expectation. At no point when she was hired was her being a cheerleader for the office ever discussed. She believed she was hired to do a job, and that's it. But because of her beautiful personality he assumed she would boost morale in the office, and for the most part she had, until recently when she was going through some shit.

If you think about it, it's a little fucked up that his first response to her change in mood wasn't to check in and see how she was doing, but to berate her performance. In reality, her performance probably wasn't affected at all, she just wasn't her happy, outgoing self.

This is what women have to deal with on a daily basis. There are so many expectations placed on women's shoulders, even without our knowledge. My friend had no idea that she was expected to be the sole morale booster in the office. She is one of the smartest, most driven people I have ever met. It's shameful that this would be expected of her. She shouldn't have been reduced to a cheerleader for the office when there is so much more that she brings to the table. She deserves better than that.

Furthermore, she was expected to boost everyone's morale when they were upset, or when things got busy and difficult at work. But who was there to boost her morale? Everyone else in the office was allowed to have low morale, but it didn't matter because my friend was there to pick them back up. No one considered what would happen if things were difficult for her. Women are expected to be happy and cheerful all the time, when in reality this isn't possible. We are often expected to take on so much in addition to the shit we already have going on. And when we do take on more than anyone can possibly handle, we are not given the support and tools we need to succeed.

Men very likely wouldn't go through something like this. Bosses don't expect men to be cheerleaders, they expect them to show up and do their jobs. So why do women have to deal with this shit? Maybe women are emotional because they carry the weight of the world on their shoulders and it still isn't enough.

The story about my friend outlines how uncomfortable men are with not only women's emotions, but women in general. There was very little attempt to find out what was wrong. The response to someone's behavioural changes shouldn't be to admonish them, but to check in with them. However, people are so uncomfortable around other people's emotions they will do everything in their power to avoid talking about them. There are men (and women, but mostly men) who don't know what to do when a woman is crying. They don't know the right words to use or how to provide comfort and support. The reason being, we've taught people to avoid emotions, and have offered little support in managing our own emotions, let alone someone else's. The workplace should be a safe space for people. They should know that their superiors have their backs, and are willing to help them get through difficult times. Again, we are all human and we are going to show our emotions. We shouldn't be expected to turn it off the second we walk into the workplace.

These feelings of discomfort extend to women in general. Some people become uncomfortable when women are not taking on a caretaker (or cheerleader) role. We think they have to do these things to earn a place in society, at the workplace, or wherever. There are some people who can't imagine women not fulfilling these typical roles, so they get uncomfortable when women don't fill them.

It's a well-known fact that some men are uncomfortable around women in positions of power. This is only because they are women; there's no other reason behind it. I guess people are just uncomfortable with women who make decisions. This discomfort causes these men to make excuses as to why they're feeling this way. They immediately jump to women's emotions as being the culprit because it's easy to latch onto and exploit. They needed to find a way to make women feel small, so they preached about all women being overly emotional until the majority started to believe it. As I said before, men are emotional as well, but some of them found the differences in the ways women show emotion and twisted it into something they could use to bully us. Again, not all men believe this and this was not the goal for a lot of men. Not every man out there is responsible for this, and it would be unfair of women to think that every single one of them was responsible. But a long time ago there were some men who had these beliefs, and it's been haunting women ever since.

I went to business school, and one day I had to do a presentation for a class so I came to school in a suit—and I say "suit" very loosely. I was wearing dress pants, a blazer and high heels. A male acquaintance of mine saw me and didn't come and say hi to me because he thought I looked intimidating. He felt intimidated because he wasn't used to being around a woman exhibiting power. This is how underrepresented women are in the workplace and in positions of power. I was still the same person. Just because I put on some fancy (ish) clothes didn't somehow magically change my personality into some crazy person. It just goes to show that even the simplest of things women do to make themselves look more powerful or professional is enough for men to be uncomfortable around them. I literally knew this person! We were in the same environment we were always in together, yet he couldn't muster up the courage to come say hi. All because I was wearing a suit and maybe walking with a bit more purpose. If this is how people we know perceive us when we appear powerful, it kind of makes you wonder what people we don't know think about us.

Another time I was participating in a case competition, which is, to put it simply, a competition where a presentation is given about the issues a company is facing and what your solution would be. I was on a team with two men. I would describe my presentation style as confident, and I would have said that one of the men on my team had the same confident style of presentation. We would practice once a week and then receive feedback from coaches. One time I received feedback that I was "too intimidating" and I needed to "smile more." The man on my team didn't receive such feedback. Our coaches were uncomfortable because I was up there confident as hell. It was a case competition. I wasn't about to stand up there, smiling like an idiot, to do a presentation. Also, I thought the age of telling women to smile more was over, but I guess I was wrong. It's also important to note I had both male and female coaches. Sometimes women are even uncomfortable with other women showing their power.

I didn't take the feedback given to me. I continued to present the way I wanted to present, because I knew I was good. I knew the other guy on my team presented the same as me, and so I wasn't about to change. And did my style of presentation win the judges over at the competition? No, it did not. We didn't even place in the top three. But I was really proud of the way I presented, and other women who watched us present had some pretty positive things to say about the way I presented. So I'll count that as a win in my books. I think people were uncomfortable because I went against their perceptions of how women normally behave. I didn't emote the way they were expecting. Rather than deliver the presentation with neutrality and modesty, I delivered it with intensity and passion.

We need to provide better education and training on dealing with emotions. People in positions of power should have appropriate responses to subordinates feeling upset. I also believe that people in positions of power should be able to show when they are feeling off as well. It starts at the top. If they demonstrate that feeling your feelings is okay, then others will follow suit. Whoever decided that leaders can't show emotions is crazy. When did acting like a human being become a bad thing? Emotions don't equal weakness. In fact, I think they show the opposite. Showing your humanity and care for other people is one of the most powerful things a person can do. It isn't natural for someone to never show their emotions, yet we act like behaving this way is something to be admired. Personally, I would love to see someone in a position of power acknowledge their feelings. This would set a precedent of people feeling safe in discussing their feelings with others. It would do wonders for individuals' mental health, and overall sense of well being. Also, this world could use a little more empathy.

We also need to accept women as powerful people. We can't get scared every time a woman gains a position of power, and we certainly can't tell them to change something about themselves so they might be more well liked. Fuck that. And if someone is uncomfortable with your emotions that's a them problem, not a you problem.

# 6
# The Tough Questions

*"A woman with a voice is by definition, a strong woman"*
*– Melinda Gates*

I once dated a guy who asked a lot of questions about what it was like to be a woman. He listened to me talk about my experiences with sexism and how it affected me, and he always wanted to know more.

One day we were out for drinks, and I told him, "My back is hurting. That means I'm starting my period tomorrow."

"How do you know that?"

"Because every time my lower back hurts, I just know I'm getting my period."

He then launched into questions about how my period affected me. He asked if it caused me a lot of pain, or if I had bad cramps. He asked if it affected me emotionally, and whether or not it could make me feel sad. Each time I gave him an answer he looked at me and listened with every ounce of his attention, not giving me any indication the topic was making him uncomfortable. I had never had such a candid conversation with a man about my period before. It was really refreshing.

The next day we went for a long walk, and I forgot to pack tampons. I told him I needed to stop at a drugstore to pick some up. I wasn't about to get a plastic bag for a single box of tampons, so I left the store without one.

"I don't really want to carry this around the rest of the walk," I said. Not because I was embarrassed about people seeing the box of tampons, but because I'm lazy.

Without a second thought he said, "Why don't we just take them out of the box and put them in our pockets?"

So, here we were. Standing in the middle of Queen Street West in downtown Toronto, hundreds of people walking by us, and he and I were both shoving these tampons into our pockets. In full view of everyone outside.

"Here, I'll find a recycling bin." I held my hand out for the empty box.

"Nah it's fine." He folded the box up and put it in his pocket. "I'll just throw it out when we get back home."

I never told him how much everything he had said and did meant to me that day. It might seem small, but I felt like he was really trying to understand me. He asked questions about the things he always knew about, but would never fully understand. I remember telling my mom about what he did because it made me so happy.

When men ask questions and try to understand women it makes a huge difference for the progression of women in society. In this case, there was no shame surrounding my period. He wanted to know if it affected me emotionally, and I knew if my answer had been "yes," there would have been no judgement. He simply would have accepted it. There are a lot of questions men could ask women, and each question asked educates them on a variety of women's issues. There really is no question too small, and women will appreciate any man's attempt to better their understanding of what we face on a daily basis.

What I saw on the street that day was a confident man who didn't give a fuck about what people thought about him. I watched him take those tampons out of the box, and nothing on his face told me he was embarrassed. I genuinely don't think he was, because he's a good man who cared about me. And that's the way it should be. Maybe if people took the time to try to understand one another the world would be a more equal place, with a lot less judgement and hostility.

It doesn't just have to be about periods either. There are a lot of topics men could ask women about to understand them better. Maybe it'll make a big difference, and maybe it won't. All I know is that for me, his small act of listening left a huge impression on me. It's something I'll never forget.

# 7

# Nasty Woman: Women in Politics

*"We need to understand that there is no formula for how women should lead their lives. That is why we must respect the choices that each woman makes for herself and her family. Every woman deserves the chance to realize her God-given potential"*

– Hillary Clinton

I am from Canada, and my whole life I have only seen male leaders elected. I have mostly seen male leaders run for office as well. I have watched the same thing happen in the United States. Neither country has ever had a woman Prime Minister or President. Yes, I know, Canada had Kim Campbell as their Prime Minister at one point, but she was only in office for four and a half months because she took over the position when Brian Mulroney went into retirement. I am talking about an elected Prime Minister, who served a term long enough to implement things on their platform. The U.S. and Canada are pretty powerful, advanced countries. It's so hard for me to wrap my head around the fact that neither country has had a female leader.

If you asked someone in North America to draw a picture of what they imagined when they saw a leader of a nation, I can almost guarantee you that they would draw a white male. This is because that's all we've ever been exposed to, and that needs to change. It's absolutely crazy to me that women make up half the population, yet neither of these nations have been led by a woman.

This is most likely because of the stereotypes I was talking about earlier. Society doesn't think a woman can handle being a national leader because she is too emotional. She will make harmful decisions because of her feelings or her out of control hormones. It could also be the equally idiotic view that women couldn't possibly be interested in politics.

The Daily Show has this segment where Jordan Klepper goes to Trump Rallies and asks the people in attendance questions. During Trump's first run as President back in 2016 one interview in particular really stood out to me — and not in a good way. Klepper asked a woman why she thought Hilary Clinton wouldn't be a good fit as President.

"A woman has more hormones," she said, "She could start a war in ten seconds. If she has hot flashes — whatever."

"Haven't all wars been started by men?" Klepper shot back.

*Silence.*

"...Yes." She finally admitted.

This is the way many North Americans view women. This narrative has been expressed countless times by both genders.

Let's first break down the belief that women aren't fit to be in office because of their emotions. Look at all the fighting going on in the world right now. The nations who are at war with one another have male leaders. These outcomes were caused when male leaders were in positions of power, and the wars continued throughout the years with different males in the same position. Yet we have heard people say women can't be leaders because their emotions might cause them to start a war. But women are not the ones responsible for starting the current wars, or the past wars. Men are. The emotional woman argument really doesn't work when you think about it in this way. Men's emotions have led to countless wars. But nobody talks about that, do they?

When I see a political leader talking about an unspeakable tragedy, I would prefer to see them showing how it affects them, rather than displaying no emotion whatsoever. If I can see they are upset, I will feel as though they might try to prevent it from happening again. If they seem unbothered by it, I think that's cause for some concern. A leader of a nation cannot be unsympathetic to the plights faced by its people. If they are unbothered, I can't help but think they don't really care. Showing empathy in a time of crisis provides comfort to people.

Jacinda Ardern, the Prime Minister of New Zealand, is a perfect example of someone who can lead a country while staying true to her humanity. She runs the country with a perfect mixture of confidence and empathy. She is more than fit to run that country, and she is doing a great job. The people of New Zealand trust her, and so they listen to her in times of crisis. This is what a leader is supposed to do. I have seen interviews where she is emotional due to tragedy, but she balances it with a show of strength. I don't know one person that perceives this woman as being weak. I also don't know one person who doesn't think she is doing a good job, despite her showing emotions.

She is praised in the media for her leadership capabilities. Empathy is such an important quality to possess in a leader, but if I asked you to name the top three qualities you think a leader should have, I don't think empathy would be up there. This is because showing empathy is often seen as a sign of weakness. It's also not something we are typically used to seeing from several of our leaders in North America. We are not accustomed to a leadership style similar to Jacinda Ardern's. Empathy should definitely be in the top three. If someone is expected to lead people and make decisions in the best interest of others, it's imperative that the individual make decisions with empathy. One has to understand people in order to make effective decisions for its people.

I wrote this book during the COVID-19 pandemic of 2020. Forbes published an article called, *What Do Countries With The Best Coronavirus Responses Have in Common? Women Leaders*, written by Avivah Wittinberg-Cox. I highly recommend reading this article. It's short and to the point, and all people, but especially women, can learn a lot. It's also a hell of a confidence booster for women who think themselves not strong enough to ever be in a position of power. Wittinberg-Cox's article explores the different approaches taken by seven different female leaders — truth, decisiveness, technology and love, and highlights that although the approaches were different, they were all effective. The approach I find most interesting is the approach taken by Norway's Prime Minister, Erna Solberg, who took the love approach. She told people their feelings were valid, and that being afraid was normal. She took a very human approach. In any sort of crisis people need to feel comforted. They need to feel like everything is going to be okay, and they need to know that the feelings they have are normal. Showing compassion and love is more effective than people think. It makes people feel like their concerns are seen, and their emotions are seen. We're so quick to discount these types of leadership styles because of this narrow belief of what it means to be strong. Love is an emotion we don't associate with powerful leadership. Maybe it's time we did.

Alternatively, the article states that the countries with the worst responses were run by men, who took a more aggressive approach. I'm not saying men are incapable of running nations at all! History shows they obviously are capable, and not all male leaders had a poor response to the pandemic. What I am saying is that it's clear women are *also* able to run countries effectively.

I think this largely has to do with trust. When a nation trusts their leader, they are going to support the decisions the leader makes for the good of their country and its people. When a nation doesn't trust their leader, they aren't going to take them seriously. When the female leaders highlighted in the article above explained their plan to mitigate the COVID-19 crisis it wasn't met with apprehension, but with a willingness to participate in a solution for the greater good of the country. This trust is likely gained because the female leaders were able to show empathy. Empathy allows people to relate to them on a personal level, and exhibiting emotions for others shows their human side. I don't believe people realize how powerful emotions can be in getting individuals to put their trust in another person.

We all saw how much people hated Hillary Clinton back in the American election of 2016. Many individuals hated her because she was a woman. I think it says a lot about how people feel about women in positions of power when they would rather have had Trump than a woman. I mean, you have a man who openly bragged about sexually assaulting women, and had women speak out about how he sexually harassed and assaulted them, yet he was still elected. Women voted for him. I don't care what the man has done for the economy, or how good of a businessman people think he is. Imagine being one of the women he sexually assaulted. They probably weren't too thrilled to see him elected into a position of power. We hold women to such little value.

Trump bragging about sexually harassing and assaulting, and degrading women is more dangerous than people realize. When someone in such a powerful position normalizes this behaviour, it gives permission for everyone to behave in such a way. It also sets the precedent that if you exhibit this behaviour, you'll get away with it. Let's pretend that it was just locker room talk for Trump. It still gives men permission to act this way towards women because they see their president doing it. Yet, the American people refused to see it that way because it was better than having a woman as president. This view of women being incapable of being high up in politics is detrimental to society.

We have seen Trump continuously bash any woman who challenges him. He has been doing this since before he was elected. He can't handle women standing up to him, and his response is often to ridicule them in some way for being a woman. He uses their gender as an excuse to speak down to them. Megyn Kelly challenged Trump about his past sexist comments about women, and his response was to say she "had blood coming out of her wherever." As if her comments couldn't be taken seriously because she was on her period, and therefore she was just being overly emotional. Although his comment was widely condemned it speaks volumes as to how men think about, and treat, women. Again, this has to do with the lack of respect we show to women, not only in politics, but in general. As a man Trump doesn't have the time for women, and he makes that very clear. We undervalue what women have to say, and it starts at the top. When Trump undervalues women, he gives permission to everyone else to do this. Therefore, the stereotypes about women can never be broken until change happens in our leadership.

Mitch McConnell, a United States Senator, was accused of refusing to take part in debates with female moderators. While he vehemently denied this claim people were quick to note that it had been over two decades since McConnell had participated in a debate with a female moderator. The fact that a female moderator hasn't been present in his debates for such a long time period is horrible in itself. Especially in this day and age. People have a right to question McConnell, and the reasons why women haven't been present when he is debating. Refusing a female moderator, or not including them in the debate process is to refuse women in politics. Perhaps what he, and men like him fear most is being outsmarted by a woman, or having a woman put them in their place. When will these men get over the idea of women not belonging in politics? It's archaic and makes no sense. Women are just as suited for politics as men are, and It's embarrassing that we have to keep proving ourselves. Women are not too emotional for politics.

I remember watching the 2016 U.S election and feeling an incredible sadness when Donald Trump won. I thought to myself, *How? Do we really value women so little as to elect this man?*

People were saying, "Well, he's going to do great things for the economy, so why shouldn't he win?" The man has repeatedly insulted, disrespected, demeaned and assaulted women. What I hear when people said he'd be good for the economy is this:

"We value the economy more than we value women."

What if your daughter, sister or mother had been someone Trump insulted? What if they were the ones he'd assaulted? Would you still want to see him standing up there?

What I saw after his election was women saying, "No more." They came together to fight to make sure something like this doesn't happen again. They raised their voices and got angry and shouted from the rooftops "WE DON'T WANT THIS MAN!" I saw women who started fighting and haven't stopped since. Trump's election ignited a fire in women that only gets stronger each day he's in office. So even though I felt sad, I also felt hope. That hope has continued to grow throughout the last four years. Women will never be silent. Not until changes are made towards a more equal world. This take-no-shit behaviour is what men like Mitch McConnell and Donald Trump inspire in women.

Breaking down the belief some people have of women not being interested in politics is difficult for me. This is mostly because it's an insane position to hold, but there are people that stand by that belief. Men and women are part of the same society. The decisions a political party makes affect both men and women, so I think it's fair to say that women, like men, have a vested interest in politics. Actually, there are stances held by political leaders that affect women more than they affect men. A woman is going to care about what a male politician has to say about women related topics. Her vote will be affected by the stance a political party holds regarding these topics—like abortions, for example. If you, as a woman, have ever held a conversation about politics it's safe to say you are interested. Don't let anyone tell you there isn't room for a woman in politics. They are wrong. Not that long ago, there were people who thought women shouldn't be able to vote. Individuals will try to justify their belief that women are not fit for office with this idea of women not being interested in politics. That's not true. They just don't want to admit their beliefs are openly sexist, so they put the onus on women. What they are really saying is women, and women's emotions have no room in politics.

I love to think Canada is a progressive country, but we still have such a long way to go. Every time I see the leaders of the Canadian parties, I'm disappointed, because I always see another man running. I have been saying for years it's time for a woman to lead this country, and I stand by it. It feels like we don't even give women any sort of consideration when it comes to a party leader. At this point I expect it to be another man. I will keep voicing the opinion that there needs to be a woman leading this nation until it happens.

What does all of this have to do with emotions? There are still people who think women are incapable of running a country. This belief centres around them being emotional, and showing their emotions. If this wasn't what people thought, we would have seen a woman holding a position of power by now. Many would rather elect someone who is entirely unqualified, rather than elect a woman. Hillary Clinton grew up around politics, and spent her life exposed to politics as well. Donald Trump woke up one day and decided to run for President. From a standpoint based on qualifications Hillary was the better option. There were people who didn't vote for her because she was a woman, and they didn't see her as fit to run a nation.

We have to stop letting men make all the decisions and pretend things are fair and equal. In order to live in a just society, we need to hear opinions from all voices. We need to have political leaders of all backgrounds and walks of life. It's time we have a woman leader in Canada and the U.S. We are still such a far way off from creating a world based on equality. A positive step would be to elect a woman leader because we deserve to have representation. We deserve to see what women can do for our country. We have seen from other countries women are capable of being leaders. They are capable of bringing about real change, and they are capable of staying strong when they need to be. Emotional or not.

# 8
# 45's Meltdown

*"Lock up your libraries if you like; but there is no gate, no lock, no bolt that you can set upon the freedom of my mind"*

*– Virginia Woolfe*

North America runs on democracy. It isn't new. How it works shouldn't be a surprise. We've seen a lot of shit when it comes to politics. What we've never seen is a president react the way Donald Trump reacted when he was not re-elected for a second term in the 2020 U.S. election. Most of the world stood by and watched, horrified, as Trump screamed, "voter fraud," and tried to overturn the results of the election using baseless and ridiculous claims. Anyone who still argues that women are too emotional to be president after Trump's tirade need to seriously reconsider this claim. That argument is no longer valid, and I never want to hear it again.

There were an alarming number of people in the U.S. who supported Trump's attempt to overthrow the election results. They blindly believed everything this man was saying, despite there being absolutely no evidence to back up his claims. The courts publicly stated there was no evidence for what he was suggesting, but people still believed the word of Donald Trump. Apparently, he is more convincing than every court in every state he tried to overturn. Untrustworthy witness after untrustworthy witness was brought forward to try and convince the world Trump was right. What we saw on the news was nothing short of embarrassing, yet

Trump raised over 200 million dollars from his followers to aid him in his challenge of democracy.

After the results of the election were announced, Trump shut himself inside the White House. He didn't address the public, he didn't congratulate Joe Biden, and he sure as hell didn't lose gracefully.

Trump's response was about as emotional as one can get, but nobody really talked about him being overly emotional about the whole thing. We don't often use the word "emotional" when discussing the reactions of men.

Now imagine if the gender roles were reversed. Imagine if it was a female president reacting the way Trump did. The public wouldn't have allowed such behaviour. It would have been used as further evidence of women's incapability to lead a country. A woman would not have received the type of support he did. If a woman had given the country the silent treatment after losing, people would have lost their goddamn minds. It would have been seen as a typical, emotional response. And she certainly wouldn't have raised 200 million dollars from people who supported her.

With no evidence of voter fraud, a woman would have been called crazy, manipulative, uneducated, unfit, emotional, and many more unflattering names.

A woman exhibiting the type of behaviour Trump did would have set women and women's rights back years. There is no room for error for women. So why do we allow men to do these things without any sort of consequence? People would never call into question a man's ability to lead after one of them royally fucks up, but one woman fucking up can derail a society's faith in all women's abilities.

Women need to walk on eggshells when they are in positions of power. The world is so unfamiliar with women in these positions that everything she does will come under intense scrutiny.

Especially when there are people in the world who will do anything in their power to keep women out of certain roles. They will use any mistake as ammunition against her. Men don't face this type of pressure from society. It's time to create an equal playing field for men and women. We need to judge them not based on their gender, but on their abilities.

# 9
# Women in Media

*"I used to be Snow White, but I drifted."*
*– Mae West*

It's no secret that women haven't always been portrayed in the best light when it comes to the media. They have had a history of being oversexualized, underrepresented, and largely given supporting roles that only serve the purpose of advancing the male lead.

I told someone I was writing a chapter on women in the media, and his response was, "Oh fuck, you could write a whole book on that topic." He's right. The media is very problematic when it comes to women, both in the way they write female characters, and how women are treated in the media business.

I have often noticed women in film being portrayed as overly emotional lunatics, while the man is calm, cool, and collected. Even in the media, women are shown to be extremely emotional, and not in a positive way. Movies such as *Saving Silverman* and *Wedding Crashers* contain good examples of crazy women, but sane men. The women in these films behave in a way that would give them the "crazy" label, but they are deliberately over the top characters. This is a very normal way to think about women, both in film and in real life. However, these are not accurate depictions of women. Where did this idea that women are crazy come from? The women in these films are mean and controlling, and then become emotional when something doesn't go their way. It leads to the idea that women are not in control of their emotions. When they feel strongly about something, they behave in an irrational manner, rather than being able to channel their emotions into an appropriate response. Seeing women behave this way in film can cause people to assume that's how they behave in real life. When you pair these films with the stereotypes people have of women in reality, it can lead to a false perception of women. We think they are crazy and emotional because the media tells us that's what women are like.

As a woman who knows a fair share of other women, I can confidently say that this is not the way we behave. I'm not saying it's impossible, but it's definitely not as common as some people think it is. I have encountered many different types of women with many wonderful qualities. It's time we start writing about and showing the positive sides of women. "Women are crazy" is such a typical thing for people to say, and it's also typical to see in film and television.

I was watching TV the other day and saw a commercial for a furniture company. In this commercial, a husband was always trying to get his wife to have sex with him, but she wouldn't do it. This couple looked like they were in their mid-thirties or so. They got a new mattress, and he finally thought she was going to have sex with him . . . and then she turned over and passed out. The scene cut to the husband, all annoyed that not even the new mattress would get her in the mood.

I really thought we had done away with the whole "women aren't interested in sex" thing a long time ago. Women are portrayed like this so often. It has led people to think that women over the age of thirty are uptight and never like to have any fun. Women enjoy a good fuck every now and again, and I'm not sure why people think otherwise. Maybe it was because back in the day women were tired of giving birth after the tenth child, and since birth control wasn't a thing, they just stopped having sex. I mean, it makes sense. At some point you've got to get tired of pushing kids out of you. But somehow that got translated into "I hate sex because I'm so uptight and joyless."

You can tell that the commercial was written by a man. He was probably thinking to himself "what a funny and original idea," when it's actually so tired. This is why it's important to have women write about women in the media: so we don't have to see stupid shit like this commercial all the goddamn time.

What may be worse is the lack of representation of women in films. When we don't accurately portray women, it hurts our understanding of them. Films and television have not historically explored female characters and their emotions. If the media were to begin making more female-centered content, we would be able to showcase how women behave in real life. Exposing the qualities women have through film is a great way for people to realize and accept how women are. If a strong and emotional woman were to be showcased through film, we might start to see how she overcomes challenges, while simultaneously dealing with her feelings. We have countless films that are entirely centered around men. Women are complex and interesting people. If we made films about them, we would get a lot of beautiful content.

We would then need more female writers and directors. The only people who can accurately portray women's stories are other women. However, Hollywood is notorious for having an abundance of male writers and directors, and only a handful of females in those same positions. Women will never be explored to their full potential in film and TV until we have more of a balance in Hollywood. There is no one better suited to explore women's issues other than women.

Since the Academy Awards began in Hollywood, the coveted Best Director award has only ever been given to one woman, and women have only been nominated for this award a handful of times.

It makes me question why women-centered films are so rare. I think it's because audiences are uninterested in seeing an all female cast. We aren't ready to accept films involving women and their struggles. We have often downplayed female emotions as trivial or unimportant. The history of women is so rich, and there are many Hollywood films that could capitalize on this, but they don't, likely because of the lack of interest from audiences. They want to make films and television that are going to sell and make money, and female-dominated films are not going to be big sellers.

Recently there was an all female remake of the movie Ghostbusters. People hated the movie before it even came out. There have been several remakes of classic Hollywood films in recent years, so why did Ghostbusters specifically receive so much hate? One can't help but wonder if it was because it was an all-female cast. Whether it was a good film or not, some individuals refused to even give it a chance. People were downvoting the film on film review websites before it was even released. The argument can be made that fans of the original were just uninterested in seeing a remake of a beloved film. However, they rebooted the Ghostbusters franchise recently as well, with a different story and different cast—this story revolves around people who discover a connection to the original Ghostbusters. The reboot has not been released yet, but it has not received the same amount of hate the remake did before it was released. The only real difference between the two films is the reboot doesn't have an all female cast.

This just goes to show how uninterested people are in seeing films with women in them. If some men were against an action/comedy starring women, there's no way they're going to want to watch a movie about women with accurate portrayals of women. We call movies with a large female cast "chick flicks" and that name has so much negativity behind it. We think they're girly movies, and we write them off immediately. But a "girly" movie isn't a bad thing. A lot of men don't want to watch movies that make you feel emotional because that's women's stuff. Even in film, men aren't ready to confront their emotions.

In some cases, the lead woman of the film is never given a proper character arc, and her only purpose is to give the audience something to look at. This is again harmful because we see women not as real people. They only exist as something to admire. Society also believes that women can't be beautiful and possess other qualities. Did you know the actress Hedy Lamar was a brilliant scientist, who made several scientific contributions to WWII? Probably not, because Hedy Lamar was a beautiful woman. If a woman is beautiful that must be all she has to offer, right?

Women aren't given the same chance as men in Hollywood. Whether we want to admit it or not, this leads the audience to see women like this in real life—that being beautiful is all they can be. That they have no other positive attributes. We are then unable to comprehend when a woman shows any sort of strong emotion or personality. I'm not suggesting that everyone sees women as lifeless robots, who can't show any sort of emotion at all. I am merely suggesting that when we don't portray women accurately in film, it warps our perception of women in real life. Therefore, we are not in tune to women's needs, which affects the way we react to their emotions.

Not all films are like this. There are films with strong female leads, and in recent years there have been some all female led movies. These are really important steps, and I'm happy we've gotten to this point. It's very likely we will see more movies like this in the future. However, we still have a long way to go in the fight for equality in Hollywood.

Accurately portraying women in film is really important. I want little girls to be able to grow up watching powerful women on screen. I want to watch powerful women on screen. Show audiences how much depth women have, and show their emotions in a positive light. All of this is possible. We just aren't giving people the chance to do it.

Another example is the 2019 film, Little Women, directed by Greta Gerwig. If you are unfamiliar with the story or film, all the main characters are female. The entire story revolves around these women. The film is brilliant. I could talk about it forever, but one thing I appreciated was how Greta Gerwig showed the emotional depth of each of the female leads. The film was nominated for six Academy Awards. I think we can all agree that's a lot of nominations, but Greta Gerwig was left out of the Best Director category. I truly don't understand how a film that had so many nominations could leave out the director. The director is the driving force behind the film. If it's nominated for six awards clearly the director has done their job and done it well. Not only do I think she should have been nominated, but I think she should have won that year! (But I'm also biased. I admire Greta Gerwig and she can do no wrong, in my opinion.)

We need to begin to recognize the importance of the role women play in Hollywood. Little Women was a beautiful film, and it was very emotional. It showed how women can be emotional and experience pain, but still make decisions in the best interest of themselves and others. It is such a wonderful example of the resilience of women, how they put others before themselves, and how capable they are of being on their own. We were given a film that honoured and accepted women's emotions without depicting the women as crazy. The film wouldn't have had the same depth if it were written and directed by a man. It wouldn't have had flawed and strong female characters if it were written and directed by a man.

We need more films like Little Women, and we need more directors like Greta Gerwig. I am entirely uninterested in a film about women directed and written by men. And I have seen enough films about men that are written and directed by men. Give women the opportunity to write about other women. It's time for women to start telling their stories. It's also time women started gaining recognition for their contributions to Hollywood. I used to avidly watch the Academy Awards. I have now boycotted it due to their lack of representation of women's contributions to film. I also hate the fact that they cater to almost exclusively white people (but that's a whole other book).

The Academy has received a lot of criticism in recent years because of the lack of representation, yet they still nominate men for the majority of the awards. Please start nominating women. It really isn't hard. Their work is just as important, and there have been several great films that have been written and directed by women. If you were asked to name five directors in Hollywood right now, I would bet every answer would be a man. Maybe after this you'd say Greta Gerwig! And I really hope you do. Learn the names of talented female directors, and maybe even try to support their films. They deserve it.

# 10

# How Underestimating Women Limits Society

*"Tremendous amounts of talent are being lost to our society just because that talent wears a skirt."*

– Shirley Chisolm

Historically, society would rather push women to the side than put in the work to create an environment that is accepting of them. Instead of trying to understand women, we have used excuses such as "women don't belong in the office," or "a woman's place is inside the home." The people who believe these things don't want to adapt, and don't really care to understand the differences between men and women, so their response is to undermine women as a whole.

As we all know, this way of thinking was very common not that long ago. And unfortunately, there are people who still believe that this is true. The people who believe this don't have time for women. If someone thinks women don't belong in business, they leave it at that. In reality, it would be much more beneficial for them to ask, "Why don't women belong in business, and how can I change that?" Maybe it isn't that women don't belong in business, but that we haven't taken the time to create a space that fully accepts women for who they are.

Let's explore this thought with an example. Say there's an office of one hundred people in which fifty of them speak only French, and fifty of them speak only English. Now let's say everything in the office was written in English. All signs, all reports, all paperwork, everything is written in English. Obviously the fifty French people won't be able to contribute much to this office. Instead of the English side attempting to adapt, and create an environment that will allow the French to be able to do the work, they say the French just don't belong. Nothing to be done about it. When, in actuality, there is so much that can be done. If they put in the work to adapt to the French speakers, they'd be able to contribute. Think about everything this office is missing out on because they won't adapt to the French-speaking side of their workforce. The English might also assume that the French people just aren't good enough to make meaningful decisions. But how can the French make meaningful decisions when their environment is doing everything in its power to work against them? They aren't being given the chance to show what they can do for the office.

This is kind of what it's like with women, except not nearly as complex. Women and men fundamentally are not that different from one another, yet these slight differences between the two do exist. It's just about understanding how women may differ from men, and believing these differences are not negative. We can choose to understand that women may show their emotions differently than men, and learn to accept it. It's also about learning how we can use those differences to our advantage. We can absolutely adapt to be more accepting of women, but we are simply choosing not to. Our world is missing out because we refuse to make a few changes.

Women's emotions have often held us back, but at no fault of our own. Someone decided they didn't like the type of emotions women exhibited and they vilified us for it. This has prevented us from doing so many things. Giving women an equal chance in this world is important and necessary. I often think about what this world is missing out on because we don't give women the chance they deserve. We've seen how the contributions of women have benefited this world, yet we still aren't allowing them to live up to their full potential.

There was a time when women weren't allowed to go to university, or work outside the home. By keeping women away from these environments, we have missed out on so much. It's actually kind of sad, if you think about it. If we went back in time and allowed women to do these things, there's a chance we could be living in a totally different world.

Growing up, when we learned about famous inventors, it was always about men. We rarely, if ever, talked about what women have done for this world. Even I am guilty of undermining women's contributions. I think we all are. In school, if we were ever discussing an inventor, in my mind there would always be an image of a man. Even today, knowing the things I know, if someone were having a discussion with me about an inventor, I would no doubt have an image of a man in my mind. When I learn about inventions, but it isn't known who invented them, I automatically assume it was a man who did it. We have failed women in this regard.

There are likely several inventions created by women, but we overlook them because of our inherent sexist beliefs. Society has taught us this is true, and now it's difficult for us to break away from having these thoughts. Moving forward, we need to create a way of learning that doesn't celebrate one more than the other. Children need to grow up thinking he *or* she could have created something. Our exclusive way of thinking is harmful because from a young age we are led to believe that historically significant events have been brought about by only men. Without meaning to, we are teaching children that we owe everything we have today to men, which affects the way we think about women as adults. We are also less likely to take the contributions of women seriously.

Some men have also been known to get credit for the contributions of women. How many women have we overlooked because of the belief that they couldn't do the same things men could? Women have been overlooked and underestimated for centuries.

The idea that being overly emotional is a bad thing has really hurt women. People assume we don't have the same capabilities as men. It's extremely frustrating. I admit that I am an emotional person. I cry easily, and sometimes I don't even know why I'm crying. But I can say from personal experience that my emotions have no bearing on my capabilities. I don't somehow magically lose all my ideas and aspirations just because I show emotion. I also don't lose the ability to have a meaningful conversation just because I might be crying. I shouldn't be taken any less seriously in conversations just because there are a few tears running down my face. And if you disagree with this statement it's because we have been brought up to believe that someone showing this type of emotion is weak.

What if instead of crying, I was getting angry and intense? The response to these emotions would be different than the response to tears—I'd be judged for showing anger, but not as much as I would for crying. It's because we are more willing to accept anger as an emotion than we are sadness. But both of these emotions are valid responses. The same goes for men in this case. If they are crying they are automatically seen as weak — because they are showing an emotion that is seen as female. When men cry society judges them for it. They aren't seen as real men, and both men and women are quick to write them off. When we don't allow men to comfortably show these emotions it is harmful to everyone. Men are not able to explore and accept their feelings, and it convinces everyone that women are lesser than men because the emotions we typically exhibit are unacceptable.

We need to change our way of thinking and accept the fact that tears are just tears. We are uncomfortable with them because we have been taught to avoid them, and to discount someone who is crying in a serious situation. Instead of discounting them, I challenge you to try to understand where that individual may be coming from. Take what these people say seriously. You may find they have some really interesting things to say. And then you never know what might come about.

I also like to think that because women feel so strongly and are empathetic, having these qualities could lead to some pretty great things for this world. Writing policies or creating things with the best interest of others in mind could do wonders for our society. We could see some real changes if we allowed women to live up to their full potential. Having emotions isn't a bad thing. It never was.

Women have been forced to adapt to a man's world. And this world taught us that being strong meant showing no feelings. It's time for this world to adapt to women. We have had enough of trying to be what other people want us to be, because what we are isn't seen as good enough. Even though we are seeing more women in positions of power, we have had to learn to adapt to a man's world. There's a good chance that even though women hold important positions, we are not allowing them to be true to themselves, because they are judged in ways that men are not. Women are scrutinized for the way they think, the way they dress, the way they feel, the way they act, and the way they look. If we stopped these judgements towards women and created an environment that is accepting of all, we may see some really great things happen. I would love to see a world that has more empathy. I would also love to see more policies and inventions created because people were empathetic towards one another. A world where men and women work together as allies.

Women make up more than half the population of this world. Encouraging women and girls to invent, and aspire to be in positions of power, could also bring about changes that directly benefit women. We understand the types of issues women face better than anyone, so who better to address these issues than women? The same can be said for men. They are also going to have a better understanding of the issues that affect them. This is why it's so important to have balance between the two. The difference is that men have always been given the chance, so the issues of men are constantly being addressed. The issues of women, on the other hand, are potentially being overlooked. We should encourage everyone to live up to their full potential, and create a world where both men and women are given an equal chance.

The bottom line is this: we need to accept women as they are, in their full emotional glory. Repressing an individual's true self because we want them to behave a certain way doesn't benefit anybody. We could truly see some really great things if we just stopped putting these ridiculous restrictions on people and just let them live their lives.

# 11
# Women, Emotions & Relationships

*"There's really no such thing as the 'voiceless'. There are only the deliberately silenced, or the preferably unheard."*

*– Aruhndati Roy*

Like most other young women, I've dated my fair share of men. Some of it has been really great, and some of it has been a goddamn roller coaster. I've been through a lot in my dating life, and at times things were really tough. But I've learned a lot about how I deserve to be treated and what I need out of my relationships. I've really tried to take the silver lining approach to dating. Even though things were bad at times, there's always something you can learn. Not in the, "I wouldn't change a thing," kind of way though. I'm happy I learned some stuff, but I would have preferred to not go through the shit I went through. In the last two years I've dated only good men, who treated me the way I deserve to be treated. I've come to the realization that these are the type of men I need to be with. It took longer than it should have for me to realize this, but life is just one long learning process. At least I came to that realization eventually!

Dating had a significant impact on my emotions. I went through a string of losers who made me feel like I couldn't be vulnerable. One of the first guys I dated made me feel really stupid the first time I opened up to him about something major that happened in my life. It was something I had a difficult time telling people, and it took a lot of courage for me to tell him. He made me feel humiliated, and even though it's been years, I will never forget that experience. I recently opened up about it to two of my close friends and they were horrified at the way he had treated me. At the time, I was too naive to see that what he was doing was a major red flag. Throughout our time together this guy would often make me feel bad about these sorts of things, so I started to hide how I felt in front of him. This set the foundation for how I would behave in my subsequent relationships.

After him, it unfortunately didn't get much better for me. For most of my dating life, men have made me feel bad about being emotional, and so I stopped telling them how I felt. It's been very difficult for me to trust and open up to men, and it's something I'm still struggling with. I realize the effect of this is I haven't been true to myself or what I wanted. When I have told men how I felt, it always seemed to backfire. And I've found that no matter how honest I was being or how much I tried to communicate, they never considered me and my feelings, or how their words and actions would affect me. I always thought I should be there for them, but never once expected them to be there for me. I never thought they'd care enough about my problems. I still really struggle with being vulnerable in front of men because of the lack of respect I was shown when I first started dating.

All of this has caused me to be really insecure in my relationships. I never felt like I could show men who I really was, or be myself around them. I felt like I was walking on eggshells because they wouldn't take my feelings seriously. I made compromises I never wanted to make because I wasn't being honest with myself about what I was feeling and what I wanted out of the relationship. There was a part of me that was so scared of getting hurt, I thought the best thing for me to do was to put up walls. I figured if I didn't let anyone in or tell them how I was really feeling, they couldn't hurt me. The joke's on me, though, because I still got hurt. Putting up those walls never did anything good for me. It actually ended up doing more damage.

In the last couple of years, the men I've dated have made me feel like I can be myself fully in front of them, and it's made such a positive difference in my life. They were really great men. I was able to open up to them about things I've struggled with or currently was struggling with. Not once was it ever met with judgement. They listened and tried to understand what it was like. I was with someone who constantly asked questions about what it was like to be a woman, and even offered up some ways in which he could have behaved differently when he had seen women being treated unequally in the past. Even though this should be the way all men think, it unfortunately isn't. It showed me what I deserve in a partner, and now I won't settle for anything less than what those men gave me. If I can't be myself in front of someone, I don't want them in my life. I don't have time for stuff like that anymore.

There's a lot expected of women in this life, and we feel this pressure to behave a certain way even in our relationships. We're expected to be there for other people, and we often end up putting their needs above our own.

I was dating this really great guy and there was one day we both had pretty bad days. For me it was really bad. I spent the whole day feeling sad and emotional. Knowing me, I had probably cried a couple of times. He sent me a message in the evening telling me he had a really bad day and asked if we could talk. The guy was upset so obviously I said yes. After we finished talking about his problems, he asked how I was doing, and my answer was, "I'm doing good! I had a good day. Nothing new to report." I lied because I knew he was going through something and I felt like I needed to be happy for him. I deemed his problem to be bigger than mine, and didn't want to burden him with what I was going through.

The thing is though, my feelings were just as valid as his. We were both going through something, but I assumed his problem was worse than mine. I didn't want to overshadow him when he was having a rough time. I was also worried about his response to my feelings. There was a part of me that thought he would think I was being stupid because my problems weren't as big as his.

This is a common response for women. We are constantly putting other people before ourselves. We give, and give, and give, and we expect so little in return. We feel like we need to be there for people, and we put our emotions and problems on hold in order to be able to do this.

In this situation, my insecurities definitely had some bearing on my ability to tell him I was feeling upset, even though this guy is a really great person. After a couple of days, I realized how silly it was of me to hide the way I was feeling from him. I told him I had a rough day a few days back, and his response was, "Oh really? What happened? Why were you sad?" I opened up to him and we talked about it, and you know what? Nothing bad happened. The world was still turning.

Not being able to be open with the person you're with means you shouldn't be with that person. It sounds obvious, but women have a tendency to make excuses for shitty men. I've done it, and I've seen my friends do it as well. We all tell each other, "Don't let that guy walk all over you. You're too good for that," and then we turn around and allow that exact behaviour to happen to us. I have made too many compromises in my life when it comes to this, and I'm not willing to do that anymore. I know what I want and need, and if they can't respect that then have a nice life!

"Women are too difficult to understand!" How many times have we all heard this one? It's the general consensus among some men out there that women are impossible. Maybe it isn't that we're difficult, and these men who think that just aren't listening.

What exactly makes us difficult to deal with? I would love to know because I've never had a man actually ask me what I want. Women make it pretty obvious what we are looking for in a relationship. Many times, it's not what men think it is either. I don't want you to buy me stuff, I want you to treat me with a little respect. You know? Some of them think buying us dinner gives them permission to treat us however they want.

A woman will outright tell their partner, "Okay I would like you to do this, this and this, and I need more of that." And then when their partner doesn't do it and the woman gets upset their response is, "Well, how could I have known? You never told me." Like, she's literally telling you what she wants, but you're just not listening. Women are not complicated. If anything, the relationship is complicated because these men aren't communicating or listening properly.

It's a vicious cycle because women tell men what they want, it doesn't happen, the woman gets upset, and this means we're too difficult and emotional. It's just another way in which we are blamed for being too emotional, or for men to think we're unreasonable. Try listening to us. A lot of the time we aren't asking for much.

There are a lot of really great men out there. It might take some time to find a good one. Like a lot of time. It's important not to sacrifice any part of yourself in order to be with someone. If you want them to respect what you want, you have to respect it yourself.

A partner who will respect your emotions is one who will also respect your boundaries. Understanding and accepting how certain things make you feel is an important quality to look for in a partner. Never compromise on this. Find someone who you can trust to accept your emotions without judgement. The more accepting they are of your emotions, the more they'll be comfortable in sharing their emotions. Communicating about your and your partner's feelings is necessary in any relationship.

## 12
# Let Toxicity Go

*"To find a prince, you gotta kiss some toads."*
*– Foxy Brown*

A few years ago I went on a date, and we hit it off immediately. This guy was funny, handsome as hell, and seemed really kind. I spent the whole time laughing with him. It was one of the best first dates I'd ever had. When I got home my roommate was in bed, but I couldn't wait to tell her about it. I went into her room, sat on her bed, and told her all about this amazing guy I had met. She and I were both really excited. It had been a long time since I'd been on a date that good. Actually, it had been some time since either of us had been on a good date.

He and I continued to go on dates. I was really happy I'd found someone I got along with so well. All of it seemed so easy with him. I had some bad luck with men in the past, and it felt really good to find someone who was actually treating me nicely. I admittedly was wary of the whole thing though because I was worried of being hurt.

Later, I was talking to my best friend about something unrelated, and I brought up how men can be horrible.

"Uh oh. Did things go south with the new guy?" she asked.

"No, not yet," I replied jokingly. "But things seem to be kind of good between us. With my track record though, I might be wrong."

"Why do you say that? Wanna talk about it?" she asked, with some concern.

She and I ended up talking about it for a little bit, and she told me everything was fine, and I was just being paranoid. I needed to stop being scared of getting hurt again, because not all men will treat me badly. I appreciated her words very much. She allowed me to get into a better headspace about the whole thing. Man, do I wish she would have been right though. Ah well. You win some, you lose some.

A little while after my conversation with my friend, this man started progressively treating me worse and worse. He was disrespectful and mean and treated me like I had no value as a human being. He started inviting me over later and later at night, and would ignore me all day. He would make plans to go on dates with me and then cancel at the last minute. Like a normal person I thought, "Let's hang out tonight," actually meant he wanted to hang out. I would tell my friends I was busy and couldn't do something with them because I was hanging out with this guy, and then get an unapologetic message about how he couldn't come anymore. Eventually I was only seeing him at two o'clock in the morning on Friday and Saturday nights. Deep down I knew he was a bad person who didn't deserve me, but he started off so great I so badly wanted to believe I was wrong.

Everyone in my life could see how awful he was, and how much better I deserved except me. He was making me miserable. I cared for him, and he knew how much I cared for him and manipulated it to his own advantage. He said all the right things and told me all the things he knew I wanted to hear because he knew it might keep me around. I fell for it for a really long time.

I spent so much time making excuses for him and wanting him to be something I knew he wasn't. The amount of time I spent trying to understand him and make excuses for him was crazy. I just didn't want him to be like every other man I had dated. I so badly wanted to be right about him that I did everything in my power to prove he was a good guy. Looking back on it, I wish I hadn't wasted so much of my time thinking about this dumbass, but here we are. I was told by everyone to get rid of him, but I had so much trouble walking away from him. I didn't recognize my own value. I also didn't recognize my own feelings. I wasn't happy. I wasn't even close to being happy. But I have this belief that everyone is good, when sometimes that just isn't true. No matter how hard I want to believe it.

One day he invited me over. I went, just like I always did whenever he wanted me to come over. He demanded so much of me, but gave me nothing in return. As soon as I walked in, he found another way to disrespect me. I finally had enough. I walked away from him and I haven't looked back. I'm happy he's out of my life. I'm a much happier person because of it. I admit that I allowed the behaviour to continue for way too long. At some point you have to realize you are gaining absolutely nothing from a relationship with someone and have the courage to walk away. It's not easy, but it's necessary.

He apologized several times to me, multiple times in person the last night I saw him, and then again by text messages over the next few months. I told him how much he had hurt me and how I couldn't take it anymore. He wasn't apologizing because he meant it. He was doing it to try and manipulate me. If I had believed those apologies and gone back to him, I know he would have continued to disrespect me. I don't know why I allowed his behaviour towards me in the first place. I really don't. Fool me once, shame on you. Fool me a hundred times, and yikes! Am I ever an idiot.

I think deep down, the reason I told my friend I was worried was because he had started to show signs that made me worried. I ignored those feelings though. I should have listened to myself instead of trying to push down the thoughts I had in the back of my mind. I probably would have avoided a lot of unnecessary pain because of it.

This man was garbage. He was using a t-shirt as a pillowcase, for Christ's sake. For a guy who was almost thirty, he sure lived like a teenage boy. That maybe should have been my first red flag. Live like a teenage boy, act like a teenage boy.

At the end of the day, I wasn't being true to myself. I ignored all the signs. And believe me, the signs were screaming at me and flashing bright red lights. Here I was, pretending like they weren't there. I was so focused on trying to find the good in him that I ignored the fact that he was causing me pain. Nobody is worth feeling like that all the time. Not everyone in your life deserves to be a part of it. If their behaviour is toxic to your own well-being, it's okay to remove them from your life.

I really do try and see the silver lining whenever something like this happens. Sometimes it's difficult to see, but there is good in every bad situation. This man showed me that I truly deserve better and listening to my feelings is really important. Since him, I've made some mistakes with men. Everything is a learning process, and sometimes you're going to slip up. Just because I had this one really bad experience doesn't mean I've learned everything there is to learn and that's it for the mistakes. There may be other slip-ups in the future. The only thing I can do is try to not let it happen to me again, and listen to the way I'm feeling. Anything less for me is completely unacceptable.

# 13
# Women Supporting Women

*"You can always tell who the strong women are. They're the ones building other women up instead of tearing them down."*

*– Anonymous*

Although the stereotypes and negativity surrounding women and their emotions were brought about by men, women need to recognize that we hold on to these beliefs about ourselves. Don't feel bad or embarrassed about it; we've been taught to feel this way since we were brought into this world, so this has naturally become our way of thinking. I admit there have been times where I've seen a woman crying in what would be considered a professional setting and felt embarrassed for her. I couldn't believe that she would allow herself to cry in such a situation.

Rather than judging her for what she did, maybe I should have been there for her. I could have stuck around and made sure she was okay, or made sure she knew that we had all been where she was. Or, if being there for her wasn't an option, I could have taken a minute to try and understand where she was coming from. Either way, this woman didn't deserve any type of judgment, and I should have known better than to judge her. We all make mistakes. I am always learning and adapting. If you have had these judgements about other women, it's completely natural. But let's all do our best to recognize this isn't okay, and take steps to change our way of thinking.

We've all been told not to cry in serious situations, so our first response to seeing someone doing this is not empathy, but embarrassment. When you put it like that, it's pretty fucked. When did we become so desensitized to people's emotions that this would be our response? Emotions are a natural part of life, and we just blatantly tell people they can't feel them. Or, worse, we tell them they should be embarrassed about feeling the way they feel. Sometimes, no matter how hard you try, those emotions are going to get the better of you. It's important to let people know that this is okay.

I was in a situation once where I had to have a very serious meeting to address an organization that I felt was taking advantage of me. I felt wronged and hurt and talking about it was incredibly difficult for me to do. I was going into this meeting alone, and talking to individuals who were very high up in the company. I knew I was going to have to say things that would be difficult for them to hear, and I wasn't sure how they would react. It was a very intimidating situation. The meeting lasted a couple hours, and at one point I started to cry. In that moment, I remember being so angry with myself. I thought up until then I had been doing a great job and making some great points, but then my emotions got in the way and derailed everything.

In fact, they didn't derail everything. The meeting went in my favour, but despite this outcome, I was still angry with myself. I had told myself before going into the meeting I wasn't allowed to cry, and I had failed. I told some of the women in my life this story. How I was such a badass in this meeting until I started crying. And then I would try to justify why I started crying, because I was still embarrassed about it. Every single woman I told this story to had basically the same response: "Well yeah, I would have started crying too." Hearing them say that held so much power for me. Knowing they would have had the same response provided comfort, and my thinking started to change. I stopped feeling embarrassed about crying. They validated the way I was feeling, and it made me feel so much better about myself.

I have also come to realize that reacting the way I did in that situation didn't make me weak. Even if I hadn't got the outcome I wanted, it was still a really difficult situation to be in. The fact I was able to walk in there and stand up for myself should have been enough to convince myself I was strong. I probably wouldn't have felt that way had the women in my life not been there for me. Surround yourself with incredible women. There are endless amounts of them out there, and no one will support you the way your friends will.

When we validate someone's feelings, it has a huge impact on them. If my friends had the opposite response to my story, it would have destroyed all confidence I had. No one will ever fully understand how much courage it took for me to walk into that meeting because they weren't the ones going through it. It's not their fault; they just weren't personally a part of it. That's why it's so important not to judge other people. If they had made me feel embarrassed or ashamed about how I reacted in that meeting, I don't think I would have the same confidence to stand up for myself like that again. And I will honestly say that meeting changed me. I became a more confident person. I was proud of how I handled what was an incredibly difficult situation, and I knew I was capable of working through anything if I were to put my mind to it. Every time a woman supports another woman, it gives her the courage to be a little more like herself. When we support other women's emotions it might make us think those emotions aren't such a bad thing. A little support can go a long way.

I remember my best friend and roommate coming home from work at lunchtime very upset. She was having a hard day at work, and she knew if she was going to stay in the office she would have started crying. She came home, had a good cry, made me cry because she was crying, and then finally started to feel better about herself. We talked through it, and I let her know everything was going to be okay, and that her crying was a perfectly fine response to her bad day.

It's so heartbreaking to me that she felt the need to come home to cry though. She didn't feel her office was a safe place for her. From a humanity standpoint, it makes no sense that she would feel the need to come home to cry. Let people be people no matter where they are! But from a pure productivity standpoint it also makes no sense she would feel the need to come home and cry. She was so overwhelmed she needed to step away from the office. If they had just created an emotional judgment free zone, she could have let out her tears, and then immediately returned to work. I want to make it clear she did nothing wrong for leaving work to deal with personal emotions. She's a strong woman, but sometimes it gets to be too much for even the strongest of women. However, having an emotional outlet at work would be beneficial for the organization and its employees. Both men and women are responsible for creating this type of environment. But I do think it's really important for women to help other women through this sort of situation.

Women aren't perfect. We don't always lift each other up, and everything is not always sunshine and frickin daisies between us. I've seen women tear other women down for no reason. I've seen women judging other women for decisions they make. There is a lot of negativity, competition, jealousy, envy, and hatred among women. We have it hard enough without needing to worry about other women trying to take each other down a peg as well.

Think about how much better things would be for us if we focused our energy on lifting each other up. How much better things would be if we took the time to understand all the great ways in which we're different. We've all been through the exact same struggles, and we've shared many of the same experiences. Making a space inside yourself to support other women is so important. The times I've felt most supported have been because of the women in my life. I think we sometimes underestimate how wonderful women really are and how kind they can be to one another.

    I was in a shop the other day and a woman politely asked if she could squeeze around me. As she walked by, she said, "I love your sweater by the way! It's so cute for fall," in the happiest tone of voice. It instantly made my day so much better. As I was leaving the shop she was driving away in her car, and she gave me a smile and a little wave. It was something so small, but I thought about the nice compliment all day. Hours later I told my friend about the nice woman in the store. Women do this all the time to one another. I have received, and given, compliments to many women I don't know. You never know what someone else is going through. Sometimes words that seem insignificant to you, might mean the world to someone else. I challenge you to give those random compliments to strangers. Tell your friends they're beautiful and smart. There's so much good in women, and they truly make the world a more beautiful place.

    Every woman has been in a position where she's been made to feel shitty about her emotions. Since we all know what it's like we need to step up and comfort each other when this happens. If your female friend comes to you and talks about her emotions, let her know what she's feeling is valid. Maybe she'll feel a little less shitty after talking to you.

## 14

# Ignore Others & Listen To You

*"Define success on your own terms, achieve it by your own rules, and build a life you're proud to live."*

*– Anne Sweeney*

When I was in junior high, we were given recommendations about which math we should take once we got to high school: easy, medium or difficult. I was always good at math and really liked it, so the toughest class was the one that interested me. I had a ninety-five percent average in my math class in grade nine. When I got my recommendation from the teacher it said I would be best suited for the medium math class. *This is a mistake*, I thought with a sense of panic. Perfect little me couldn't imagine not being recommended for the most difficult class.

Because I was in such a panic about it, my parents set up a meeting with my math teacher to talk about why I was recommended for the medium level of difficulty when I had such a high mark in the class.

"She asks too many questions," my teacher said simply.

My parents looked at one another. "Okay. Isn't asking questions a good thing though?"

"No, because it means she doesn't understand the material fast enough," my teacher answered.

"Yes, but she still understands the material. Why does it matter how long it takes her to get there?" I could see them trying to understand the logic behind what this woman was saying.

"I just think she belongs at an easier level. I stand by my recommendation for her," she said with finality. She wasn't rude about it, but it was clear she wasn't open for a discussion about it either.

As we left the school my mom and dad said to me, "That was stupid. Don't let her make you think you can't do the most difficult one. You can do whatever you want. If you want to take that math class, then take the math class. If you're asking questions, maybe she's not teaching the class the way you need to be able to understand it quickly."

You know what? They were right. That was a stupid thing to say. We're often convinced there is only one way to do something. One speed to do something. And everything that falls outside of the expectations is wrong. It's a good thing my parents have always encouraged me to do what I feel is best for me. What I think and feel is the most important feedback I could receive. If I felt I was capable, then goddamn it, I was capable.

I took the math class. I passed the math class. I went on to study and graduate with an accounting degree from university. I knew I would have had success if I took this class. I was glad I listened to my feelings and not listened to information designed to hold me back. The only person who knows whether or not you can do something, or whether or not you want to do something, is yourself.

This teacher had no impact on my life. I don't remember much about her. I don't remember her being a particularly good or bad teacher. I doubted my abilities because she doubted them, and I was willing to wholeheartedly listen to her and what she felt about me. Why was I so willing to accept this? Why did I have so much doubt in myself over someone who I never respected that much? It's because she had a position of power over me, so I was ready to accept it, even though in the back of my mind I knew it was wrong. She was entitled to her opinion, but at the end of the day I should have had faith in what I knew I was capable of.

Listening to and honouring your feelings will guide you and shape the world you live in. To ignore those feelings is foolish. The person who understands you best will always be yourself. It's important to not put too much stock into what other people have to say about you. You certainly shouldn't limit yourself or hold yourself back based on someone's advice. Especially a teacher from junior high who didn't take the time to know you or understand you as a person.

# 15
# The Angry Woman

*"What a bitch!"*
– Men, whenever they
encounter an angry female

I remember a close friend of mine telling me a story about an experience she had with a pissed off customer, back when she worked in customer service. She was sixteen at the time, and she couldn't give a customer what he wanted. He wasn't challenging a policy of the organization, he was trying to challenge a law. She told him why she wouldn't be able to give him what he was asking for, and he kept challenging her on it. She was very adamant that she would be unable to process his request, and she was telling him with finality there was nothing she could do about it. His response was to tell her that she "[was] being a huge bitch," and storm off. Keep in mind my friend was sixteen, and this was an adult male throwing a tantrum because she wasn't LEGALLY allowed to give him what he wanted.

Some men throw the word "bitch" around whenever they are dealing with a difficult woman. This customer didn't like that this young girl was telling him "no," so he responded by calling her names. She wasn't actually being bitchy or rude, but because she was being strong his brain told him "woah, what a bitch." Some men take issue with being told off by a woman. They don't expect it or want it to happen, so they freak out when it does. Imagine calling a sixteen year old a bitch when you're a forty year old man.

I can promise you it doesn't make you look tough. It makes you look like an idiot.

These men are also quick to throw "bitch" around when they encounter a woman who they perceive as speaking angrily. There are men who can't fathom women being justifiably angry, so they brand women as being hysterical or bitchy when they do get pissed off. They do this in order to try and diminish the way women are feeling. When men get angry, we don't brand them as anything. We just allow it to happen without any judgement on their character.

I also believe that some men perceive certain behaviour in women to be anger when it isn't. If a woman speaks passionately about something, she may be called a bitch. A passionate woman is a dangerous woman, and people will sometimes confuse passion for anger. Calling a passionate woman a bitch is actually a pretty good tactic if you want people to discount what she says. If people think she is getting hysterically angry they'll take what she has to say less seriously. So some men have fooled society into believing that any show of emotion from a woman is a bad thing. We also have this idea in our head that women usually keep their heads down and won't fight back. When they do get angry and fight back, people aren't used to it. This surprise leads us to believe things about women that aren't true. However, we've seen enough powerful women in this world to know that they aren't being bitchy when they're angry. Unfortunately, not everyone sees it this way. If we've allowed men to get away with this show of emotion for this long, we have to allow women to do it too.

I can't think of a super strong label we give to men when they are being emotional. Maybe we call them a pussy, but that's only if they are showing a typical female emotion. If they are showing anger we may call them an asshole, or a dick. However, those words wouldn't define a man, even if he was in a high position of power. If they are called an asshole people would be really quick to forget about it, or write that label off. Men are judged differently than women, so those labels tend not to haunt them for their entire fucking careers. But if a woman in a position of power were called a bitch or emotional it would follow her around forever. Fear of these labels cause women to behave differently than they normally would. We are not seeing women's true selves. A lot of us hide or change who we are because it may make men uncomfortable, or it might piss them off enough to try and ruin our names.

Ladies, have you ever been asked out by a man and when you turn them down their response is "you bitch"? Because I have—several times. It most recently happened to me when I was walking down the street. A man tried talking to me, and I told him I wasn't interested. He wouldn't take no for an answer, so I got a little forceful with my response. He didn't like my response, so he called me a "stupid bitch" and his friend called me a "dumb cunt." Call me crazy, but I think calling me a "cunt" might have been a bit much. These men lost their shit when I became the slightest bit angry. They didn't appreciate me a) saying no, and b) standing up for myself. It made them uncomfortable.

I was scared because their response was so aggressive, but looking back on it, I'm more embarrassed for them. We've all heard horror stories of what happens when some men don't hear what they want to hear. It's very common, and it's something that almost all women have had to deal with at some point in their lives. When these men don't get their way, they throw an adult tantrum, and resort to name calling, or worse. Responding in this way makes them look like complete idiots.

Some men don't like when they can't bully women into doing what they want. In the past they were largely able to get away with it, and now that we're no longer allowing them to do this it means they need to come up with new strategies. When we use the word "bitch" in response to a powerful woman being powerful, we're trying to take some of that power away from her.

Alexandria Ocasio-Cortez, the current U.S. representative for New York, made headlines recently when a congressman called her a "fucking bitch" as they were leaving chamber. She made an impassioned speech that ended up flooding social media. In her speech she talked about why this language is unacceptable and needs to stop. If you haven't seen her response to this congressman, I suggest you try to find it. She is a young, democratic woman who is known to stand up for what's right. She is constantly challenging societal flaws, and she's bringing awareness to many issues. Some men don't like her because of this. Their response to this powerhouse of a woman is to call her a bitch because that's all they can do to fight her right now.

Some men have such a hard time accepting that women are starting to be noticed, and are starting to make some real changes. They're scared, and they're lashing out. Women aren't as easy to control as they once were, and "bitch" doesn't hold the same weight as it used to, because women aren't allowing it to define them anymore. We are taking power away from that word. However, it's still an unacceptable way to describe a woman showing anger or passion. Passionate women are changing the world. And as Alexandria Ocasio-Cortez said, "bitches get things done."

Our society has taught us that it's okay to call challenging women bitches. We don't think twice before doing it, both men and women alike. I know that women aren't innocent in this. It's just another product of our upbringing. Men used it to describe strong, confident women and it stuck. We grew up seeing it happen, and we are still seeing it happen. It's not fair to women.

Women can't win. When we show anger or sadness, we're too emotional. When we don't show enough emotion, we're cold and heartless. Society expects women to fit into this thin margin of emotion. When we go outside of it, we are crucified for it. But I say get angry. You should be angry. We've been dealing with this shit for way too long, and it's time changes were made. I'm angry. I don't have as big of a voice as others, but I know I still have a voice. I'm going to use it as much as I can until I start to see some changes. A lot of small voices can lead to big things.

The amount of powerful women right now is overwhelming the misogynists. We are fighting and they don't like it, so they are hellbent on doing everything they can to stop us. Unfortunately for them, we've started the fight, and there's no way we're stopping it now.

# 16
# Fear Conqueror

*"Angry women care. Angry women speak and yell and sob their truths."*

– Roxane Gay

My acting class really opened my eyes to a lot of lies I had been telling myself. It allowed me to open up and feel things I had previously pushed down. One day I was working on a scene, and my acting teacher told me I wasn't being honest with my emotions in the scene.

"I think you want to get angry," she observed.

"Mmmm I don't think that's how I'm feeling right now." I didn't really take the time to listen to my emotions.

"No, I think you do. I really think you do. Why are you not getting angry?"

I shrugged, genuinely not knowing why I was avoiding anger in my acting.

She looked me dead in the eyes and spoke the words that would change the way I thought about myself and my ability to show anger, "It's because you're scared."

At first when she said it, I thought she was crazy. *I'm not scared to show anger, that's ridiculous.* But the more I thought about it, the more I realized she was right. Then the panic set in because I knew I'd have to tell everyone what I was thinking, and I knew she would make me address this fear. *Oh God. In front of everybody.*

"Yeah, I think I am," I apprehensively admitted to her and everyone in the room.

"You've spent your whole life avoiding anger because that's what you've been taught you have to do," she explained. "This is very common among women."

It really hit me how much I was scared to show my anger in front of other people. Even if it was just in my acting. She worked with me to try and get me to show that side of myself, but I could tell I was holding myself back. There was no way I was going to be comfortable enough to get angry in front of all these people.

From that point forward she really encouraged me to explore these emotions I had previously hidden from so many people. She worked with me and encouraged me to understand anger wasn't a bad thing, and feeling my feelings was necessary in both my acting and in my personal life.

Life is messy, and I needed to start showing people the messy sides of me. I'm not this perfect little woman who never gets worked up over anything. No woman is. I had been denying this side of my personality for my whole life because I thought that's what society wanted from me.

Once I realized I was repressing these emotions, I actually found it very easy to explore. I gave myself permission to be vulnerable in front of people, and to show my anger if I needed to. It took work, and it definitely wasn't something that happened for me overnight. I learned what worked and didn't work for me. I thought meditating might help, but I was never able to get into it. I always found my mind would race, no matter how much I tried to reel it in.

For me it was reassuring myself it didn't matter what people thought about me. When I found myself feeling overwhelmed or anxious about it, I started saying something positive to myself over and over. Something simple like, "It doesn't matter what people think. Your emotions are valid." I would say these things in my mind until I started to calm down. I began to use this practice in my everyday life, especially when I was anxious or if things were bad. Saying these small reassurances have more of an impact than I thought they would.

*Everything will work out for you.*
*It's all going to be okay.*
*It doesn't matter. Don't turn it into something more than it is.*
*It's okay. You're going to get through this.*

Repeating these things to myself grounds me. When I find myself spiralling into negative thoughts, saying these things removes some of the weight I put on myself. I can feel myself breathe better and start to relax.

Over the course of the next few months, with work from my teacher and myself, I was able to get to a place where I was able to be angry. It wasn't as scary as I thought it would be, and I really went for it. Anger doesn't always equal yelling or screaming either. There is no correct way to show your emotions. Just feel what you feel, and it will present itself in the way that's best for you.

At the end of class, we always did this really nice thing where we would give a compliment to someone for the work they showed in class. A lot of the people gave their compliments to me that day. They knew it was hard for me, and they recognized my success. It felt great to hear those words, and it was comforting knowing there were so many people in my corner. Wonderful things happen when we allow people to be their true selves without passing any judgement. Anger might not seem pretty, but when you look past the surface of it, you'll see it's more about people expressing who they are and how they feel.

Anger is not as scary as it seems. Allowing myself to feel really angry has led to some pretty cool things. I never would have written this book had I not allowed myself to feel really angry and express those feelings I had swimming around inside me. If I had never had that angry conversation with my mom about these issues, I don't think this book would exist right now. I went from hiding my anger to telling everyone who picks up this book, "Hey I'm feeling pretty angry about the way women are treated. I want something to be done about it." So here I am. In all my anger, admitting to everyone how I feel. And you can do it too.

# 17
# Feeling the Pressure

*"I do not wish [women] to have power over men; but over themselves"*

– Mary Wollstonecraft

Women are under constant scrutiny, expected to be a version of themselves that's impossible to achieve. We have to look age twenty for our whole lives, be thin, get a good job, get married, have kids, take care of the kids while working full time, be nice, be respectful, have big boobs or a big ass (otherwise we aren't real women), take care of other people's needs, be everything society says we should be . . . the list could go on forever. It's exhausting. Men don't face the same type of pressure women face every single day. They can't begin to imagine how taxing it is on women and girls to stare this in the face literally all the time.

When society constantly tells women they aren't good enough, it's going to have a negative effect on our emotions. We are constantly comparing ourselves to other women and wishing we could be something we might never be.

There are some days I wake up and I feel shitty about myself or where I'm at in my life for no reason. There are days I wake up and I'm super confident, and other days I wake up hating everything about the way I look. When I have those shitty mornings, it affects the way I conduct myself for the rest of the day, even on a small scale. If you start the day off feeling bad, it's really hard to get that feeling to fuck off. We've all been there, and there's nothing wrong with it.

Ladies, how many of you have a pretty consistent monologue going in your head about what people are going to think about you? Mine is there all the time. There are times in my life I'm way more insecure than others. Sometimes I'm comfortable with the way I look, and then there are days where I look in the mirror and think, *Wow you are not cute*. When I'm having those insecure days, my thoughts can turn really negative. I'll go out for dinner and stress about what I should eat because I'm concerned I might gain weight. And then I'll think about all the things I ate earlier in the day for no other reason than to stress myself out about eating. If I know I'll be having a big dinner on the weekend, I worry about eating that much food in the days leading up to it.

This way of thinking is insane, and I know it's insane. I try not to let these thoughts hold me back. If I want to go out for dinner, I'm going to go. And I'm certainly not going to let these feelings stop myself from going into a food coma at Thanksgiving. But these feelings are there. It sucks because I know it's also preventing me from enjoying myself to my absolute fullest. No matter how hard I try to shake these feelings, I can't do it, so I've learned to live with it. These thoughts aren't controlling my life or what I do. I am still able to enjoy myself, but I really want to get to a point where this isn't the first or second thing I think of when I am having my bad days.

Men don't have that problem to the degree that women do. I don't want to diminish men's insecurities, because those insecurities exist and they are valid, but women deal with it regularly on a much larger scale. Men usually aren't too concerned about what people will think about their black t-shirt and jeans. But a t-shirt and jeans for women is not as simple as it sounds. Should I tuck it in my jeans? Should I knot it? Should I pair it with a belt? What jewelry should I wear with it? Part of it is wanting to look nice, but for me I want to wear what will make people judge me the least as well. So a bunch of thought goes into the most simple of things.

Men usually joke about how long it takes women to get ready before going out. They think it's a vanity thing, but there's so much more behind it. We get ready because we're always judging ourselves and comparing ourselves to other women.

I went out with my best friend one day, and she is a beautiful woman. I'm not biased either, she is very attractive. She was wearing this really nice floral print fall dress, and she paired it with a jean jacket and little black boots. Her hair was lightly curled, and she was wearing the tiniest bit of make-up. I thought she looked gorgeous, and she did. Anyone who saw her would have told you she looked really pretty. We had dinner reservations, but we stopped in for a drink at a different restaurant beforehand.

When we finished our drink, she asked me really sheepishly if we could stop back at her place so she could change. She really wasn't feeling confident in her dress and she wanted to put on something else. She kept apologizing, but I've been in her exact position before, so I was of course okay with stopping for a quick outfit change. It didn't matter that I thought she looked beautiful, and it wouldn't have mattered if everyone else in the world thought she looked beautiful. She didn't feel that way, and the only way she was going to feel better was by putting on something else. I know those feelings were playing in the back of her mind the whole time we were out for that drink. I also know my friend couldn't fully enjoy herself because of these feelings.

I have never been out with a guy who needed to go home because he didn't feel confident in his outfit. Ask the men in your life when the last time they felt this way was. We all know what the answer will be. It isn't because they naturally have more confidence than us, it's because society doesn't have them questioning their looks every second of the day. Sadly, this is how women feel all the time. It will govern our lives no matter how badly we don't want it to.

The amount of pressure women face to look a certain way is crazy. We have to fit our outward appearance into this really small box of what's acceptable. We walk down the street and are blasted with images of photoshopped women and we want to look like them. We know that when we go for a job interview, one of the first things we'll often be judged on is our attractiveness. We step outside and wonder what people will think about the way we've dressed. Going to the beach is a fucking nightmare for some women because they think their bodies don't fit society's narrow box. It's hard! If you think about it, it kinda makes sense that we'd be emotional all the time. We look in the mirror and feel anxious every goddamn day.

I used to worry about whether people I had never met before would like me or not. So I would be super careful meeting them for the first time to try and gauge what kind of person they would like. I found I was doing this mostly around men. I'm a pretty loud, in your face kind of person, and I was worried they wouldn't like it. For a time, I thought that wasn't what most women were like, so men wouldn't be used to me. Which I know is super dumb. So I would tone it down in front of them, even as I became more comfortable with them. As I get older my attitude has changed to a more "fuck it" way of thinking, and if they don't like me for me, then I don't care. I've really tried to be unapologetically myself these last few years, and so far, it's going pretty well.

Once I had a guy tell me "you're not like other girls." My response was "thank you." Why would that have been my response? Is it so bad to be like other women? What? Women are amazing and I should have been insulted when he told me that. There's all this pressure on girls to be like every other woman, but society gets offended when we aren't completely original.

Women face so many challenges on a day-to-day basis. Always thinking you aren't good enough is a pretty awful feeling. There's this constant need to prove ourselves to others, especially men. If you stopped to consider what we actually have to deal with it's no wonder we're emotional sometimes. I mean, Jesus Christ, of course women have a lot of feelings. Everything we do is constantly scrutinized! Think of what this does to a person emotionally. It's draining.

Working your ass off to grow and build yourself into the person you are, but never being good enough, is hard. We're going to feel a range of emotions because of this. Men don't get an opinion on women's emotions when they don't experience the same pain and hardships we do. They can't imagine what it's like for us, so they don't get to dictate how we respond to things. If we're emotional we have every right to be. Life isn't always easy for women. Let us handle it the way we need to.

## 18
# Superstar

*"I am a woman with thoughts and questions and shit to say. I say if I'm beautiful. I say if I'm strong. You will not determine my story—I will."*

*– Amy Schumer*

All my life, I have wanted to be good at everything. If I tried something new, I had to be good at it. I would sometimes work myself to the bone trying to prove that I was good at everything. If I wasn't good at something it would drive me insane, and I would think about how unfair it was that I couldn't get it.

I dipped my hands into so many different things; sports, arts, academics, you name it and I wanted to try it. This isn't a bad thing. I think it's important to try as much as you can to determine what you like. The problem for me was many of the things I tried I didn't like, but I continued with them until I felt I was good enough to say I mastered it. I've always had this weird need to prove myself to others. I've felt like if I wasn't good at everything I did, then I wasn't good enough at all.

I felt like there was this fire inside me. No matter how much I added to this fire, it never burned enough. I could always add more. I could always be more. So I pushed and I pushed, and I added and added hoping to be everything I could be. I never stopped to think that maybe I was burning a little too hot. I was exhausted from trying to make myself into something unsustainable. I let that fire burn out of control.

On the flip side, if I was good at something and others said I was good at it, I felt like I could never stop doing it. I thought I would disappoint people if I stopped doing something I was good at. I did things I no longer enjoyed doing because I was worried about what people would say if I stopped doing them.

I have spent so much of my life caring about what other people will think, and for a long time I didn't consider my own feelings. It didn't matter that something didn't make me happy anymore. It made other people happy, so I would keep doing it.

I've realized this is a really stupid way of thinking. There are always going to be people who judge you, no matter what. If you let those people get to you, it'll take over your whole life. It was taking over mine. Not only was I doing things I didn't enjoy, but I was constantly worried about what other people thought about me. I used to get embarrassed for not being good at something. What an exhausting way of thinking.

It's okay to be selfish sometimes. I have a friend who constantly reminds me that I'm allowed to do things for me because she knows the way I am. Sometimes I need the reminder, but for the most part I've really started to do what I need to do. I've started to let go of that incessant need to please everyone. I still worry about it. I think we all do, to some degree, but I've decided to live my life the way I want to live it. To do the things I want to do. If someone doesn't like it, that's fine. It isn't their life to live. If they're judging me for how I choose to spend my time, maybe they have too much time on their hands. I have no room for that kind of negativity in my life anymore.

It's also okay to do something and be bad at it. If you enjoy it, do it. There's no law that says you have to be good at something in order to keep going with it. If you want to write a crappy song, write the crappy song, and sing it at the top of your lungs. Does your painting look like a five year old did it? Great. Hang that shit with pride. Dance your heart out even if you have two left feet. I'm not good at everything I do. That would be impossible. There are things I do that I will probably never be great at, but I enjoy doing them, so who cares.

We determine our own happiness. Life is too short to do things for other people. And life is certainly too short to do something you don't like doing. It's a good thing to take risks and try things you might never have done before. Go outside your comfort zone and you might surprise yourself.

Find the things that make you happy, and stick with them. And if you ever find something isn't bringing you the same joy it used to, there's nothing wrong with moving on from it.

# 19
# No

*"You can be a good person
with a kind heart and still say no."*

*– Lori Deschene*

I think every woman should look in the mirror and practice saying, "No." Do you know how many things I've done because I was too afraid to say no? Or how many people I was afraid of hurting if I said it? Oh god, the list would be endless.

You are not obliged to do things you don't want to do. I am so bad for saying "yes" to absolutely everything. There was this really toxic person in my life who would ask me to do things for her all the time, and every single time I would say yes, because I didn't want to disappoint her. She was taking advantage of me. I knew she was, yet I still had this need to help her.

One day, I came home after helping her with something and started bitching to my roommate about how she treats me like shit.

"Why don't you just not do it?" My roommate asked. "Don't do things for her if she's like that to you."

"I feel bad though, she needs me. I can't just stop helping her, she'll know I don't like her," I stupidly argued.

"And?"

And.

That one word really got me thinking about all the times I'd done things for people I didn't want to do. More importantly, I started thinking about the things I'd done for people who didn't even treat me nicely.

I said to myself, "The next time she asks you to help her, you have to say no."

A little while later she asked for my help again, and you know what I said?

"Yeah, for sure! I'll be there." Dear God. What an idiot.

I never said I was perfect at all this stuff. You can't change overnight. I was kicking myself for saying yes. The next time she asked me to do something I said yes again. I couldn't help myself. I was so used to saying yes for everything, the thought of saying no was really scary for me.

It took a while, but I did stop saying yes to this person. I listened to my feelings and took my own happiness into account. Helping her brought nothing good into my life. If anything, it made me feel really bad about myself. Saying no to this person was the best thing I could have done. Listen to your feelings and honour them.

I wasn't listening to what I wanted. I instead put everyone else's feelings before mine, and I was wasting my time doing stuff I didn't want to do. Even if you like someone, you are allowed to tell them you don't want to do something. You are incapable of pleasing everyone all the time, so why bother trying?

It's a common problem for women to feel the need to please everyone all the time. We feel like we have to take care of everyone. You are just as important as everyone else, and self care should be a priority. You're hurting yourself by always agreeing to everything that's asked of you. If you don't want to do it, then don't do it. The other person isn't going to die just because you've told them no. They'll get over it.

Every woman should practice saying that small but scary word in the mirror over and over again. Watch yourself be that badass bitch when you say the word out loud.

*No.*

*No.*

*Fuck, no.*

*No.*

Too often women sacrifice their own well-being for other people. Take care of yourself. You're worth it.

# 20

# What Are We Afraid Of?

*"When I'm sometimes asked 'When will there be enough (women on the Supreme Court)?' and my answer is: 'When there are nine.' People are shocked. But there'd been nine men, and nobody's ever raised a question about that."*

*– Ruth Bader Ginsburg*

I would love to live in a world where men and women are completely equal. A world in which I wouldn't have to celebrate a woman elected as president, because it's become such a normal thing to happen. It's hard for me to wrap my head around how much of a man's world we're actually living in. And this is with progress! How much more do women have to prove themselves in order for us to get a little fucking equality?

If we allowed women to be themselves with full acceptance and no judgement, they would gain a lot more power. Many of the roles that historically went to men would now have to be shared with women. Some men have become so used to living in a world that puts them first, they are unsure about losing what they have. They don't want to have to share with women, and they don't want the competition. Throughout history, it's been easy for them to get jobs and gain high ranking positions of power. Up until recently, they never felt threatened by women because there was no chance of one taking a position away from them. Women aren't interested in being sidelined anymore, and knowing the changes that are coming is causing men to feel threatened.

But really, what are we so afraid of? What's the worst thing that could happen in creating equal representation? For some men, it's a fear of losing control. Typically, women have been seen as easier to control, so they were easier targets. In oppressing women, men were able to create a world in which the decisions were exclusively theirs. The problem with this was women got fed up, and they got fed up fast. As women gain more power, we are demanding changes be made. Changes that will directly affect men and the amount of hold they have on this world.

It makes sense though. Think about it. If you grew up in a world where things were handed to you, you would be a little bummed if someone said they wanted to take that away. I know I would. Men created a world that benefited them, and they have continued to reap the rewards of this system for way too long. It's difficult to give something up after you've had it for such a long time.

If you were in their position, you probably would have done the exact same thing. You wouldn't have challenged a system that benefited you so greatly. Men never saw a problem because they were never affected. Deep down, a lot of these men know women are making good points and good strides towards making change. They just don't want to lose their positions within this system because they are so comfortable within it.

We can't really imagine women holding a majority of elected positions, or women holding the majority of the positions on company boards, because it's never been a reality. Why couldn't that happen though? It would be great if we could get to a point where this wouldn't offend or shock people. If women are qualified for these positions, let them have them. And if it just so happens that there are more women in these positions at times, that's fine.

Women are held back because of inherent sexism. Some men truly believe women are not capable of doing the same things they are. Besides being ignorant, these men are fragile. The thought of women holding the same amount of power as them is a threat to that fragile masculinity, and it scares them. They know there's a good chance they could lose out to a woman, and they aren't ready for that. They also aren't ready to accept they might have to work with a woman who is in charge. They are horrified at the thought of taking orders from a woman, or a woman telling them what to do.

Fragile masculinity is a huge issue in society. It forces men to think they have to be a certain way, and if they don't adhere to it they aren't good enough. Many of the issues both men and women face are a direct result of telling men they have to be tough and strong all the time, and aren't allowed to show any emotion. They've been brought up believing they have to be the decision-maker and make more money. We've made a lot of progress, but there are still men who would be embarrassed that their wife makes more money than them. Many men and women would judge a man for staying home with the kids while the wife goes out and works. Why is this so controversial? Who cares who stays home with the kids? When we judge them for these decisions we contribute to the belief that men are incapable of raising their own children effectively. We also perpetuate the belief that there are certain roles that belong to men, and certain roles that belong to women. And a man taking on a "womanly role" is something to be embarrassed about. All of this contributes to fragile masculinity. Any activity that is perceived as a threat to their masculinity will cause some men to run as fast as they can away from it.

Men are fragile despite this tough wall many of them hide behind. The ones who can't accept their fragility are the ones who are going to lash out at the prospect of women being treated equally. These men need healing, and we all have a responsibility to ensure they have the resources to get to this point. It might not be easy for them, and the thought of giving up this comfortable life they've become accustomed too might be difficult to accept. They've believed for centuries that this is the way things should be, and they won't change overnight. The best we can do is keep the conversation going and keep fighting for a more equal world. And show them it isn't that scary after all.

What these men haven't done is stop to think about the benefits of equality. They should be excited about all the new and exciting things that are going to come from giving women more opportunity. They take these changes personally, though. They see it as having a negative effect on them specifically, and they aren't thinking about the broad picture. They're also operating with blinders on. It's not about being unable to see it, it's that they don't want to see it. They are so opposed to women gaining more power, despite the evidence that is being thrown at them.

Some men are afraid because they don't understand women, even though they might try to. Rather than keep trying, they chalk it up to women being impossible to deal with. A lot of these feelings revolve around some men's inability to connect with women's emotions. A lot of men have been taught not to show emotions and therefore don't know what to do when someone has them. They've also been incorrectly taught that women are emotional all the time. So the thought of dealing with this constantly is a scary thought for them.

It made sense for men to feel this way back in the day. It had been drilled into their heads that women are emotional and aren't up for handling massive amounts of responsibility. However, women are showing this is untrue, and there's plenty of evidence telling these men it's untrue as well.

The men who still believe this to be true are the ones who don't want to see women in power. Women's emotions can be used as an excuse to fight against change. These men need to find ways of making people think women aren't up to these tasks because they are unable to accept things are changing. They're latching on to anything they can in order to try and save a system that has provided them with so many benefits. The men against these changes use several excuses. Targeting a woman's emotions is just one of them.

Women are pretty amazing. I love women. I think men, for a long time now, have also begun to realize how great women are. The only two responses to this are to either accept it or don't. I know a ton of men who are fully embracing the idea of women gaining more power. It doesn't scare them at all.

So I say, let's get more aggressive! We need to keep pushing for more equality. Both men and women should keep fighting until we are seeing an equal number of men and women in positions of authority. This will benefit men as well, even though some of them might not see it this way.

# 21
# Men & Their Emotions

*"A woman needs to know but one man well
to understand all men; whereas;
a man may know all women and not
understand one of them."*

– Helen Rowland

If we are going to have an open and honest conversation about women's emotions with men, it is important to recognize that men have had their own issues with society judging them for their emotions. They are victims of a harsh, and sometimes, unforgiving society as well. Addressing men's emotions and why they might feel so strongly against showing them is important. Men are not the bad guys. Society is. To blame all men for the issues women face surrounding their emotions would be completely unfair. Just as society has done a disservice to women surrounding their emotions, it has done the same thing for men. The good news is, men can unlearn what society has taught them about emotions, and what it means to be a man. It's not going to be a walk in the park, but it also isn't impossible.

When it comes to emotions, I feel bad for men. I really do. So many of them have been brought up to believe they aren't allowed to show them. And "being a man" is the only thing that's important in life. Men have emotions, and they have a lot of them. Just because they've been told to hide them doesn't mean they aren't there. Men hide their emotions, and think that just because they cover them up it makes them disappear. Out of sight, out of mind, is not the correct attitude to adopt when dealing with emotions. When someone doesn't address their emotions, or learn to deal with them, they can manifest into unhealthy emotional behaviour. Bottling shit up is bound to take its toll on someone. Eventually it'll explode and has the potential to cause a lot of damage to that person, and the people closest to them. Simply recognizing that men have emotions and making them feel as though they can be open about them has the potential to make a big difference.

I've been really lucky in that I've had a lot of supportive people in my life. If ever I felt like I needed to talk, there would always be someone there to listen to me. I've tried to be there for people that have needed it as well. Talking about my emotions with others feels therapeutic to me. It allows me to vent and get my frustrations out. I have also cried countless times in front of my girlfriends, and never have felt judged by them. I also have what I call "the shower cry." Sometimes I feel like I need a good cry, and I get the most release in the shower. So I'll hop in there for thirty minutes, knowing that I will have a borderline breakdown, and when I get out I feel so much better. Having all these different outlets allows me to manage and deal with my emotions. I don't know what it's like to bottle my feelings up and feel like I can't go to anyone.

For a lot of men, this is a sad reality. Growing up in a world that teaches them that they have to hide their emotions can be very isolating. They don't have the same outlets we have, and a lot of men don't feel like they can go to their friends and have a serious, emotional conversation. They likely don't even allow themselves to show their feelings when they're alone. They wouldn't have a thirty-minute shower cry, because even alone they feel the need to maintain this masculine persona.

We've been teaching them to hide their emotions, so it's not really a surprise when we encounter men who don't feel comfortable around a woman's emotions. We've been drilling into their minds that emotions make someone weak. We haven't convinced women of the same thing, so it was automatically assumed women were weak.

Teaching boys that feelings are bad has negatively impacted both men and women. We don't respect men who cry, and we don't respect women at all. We've created a false perception of both women and men, how they should be, and what they are capable of.

Women and men have an equal responsibility in making boys and men feel comfortable in showing their emotions and talking about their feelings. It's a two-way street. We don't check in on our male friends enough, and we don't have conversations with them about how they're doing emotionally. They deserve our support as much as anybody else. Reaching out to them more and encouraging them to talk about their feelings may help them open up. Even if they don't it's nice for them to know that someone is there for them if they need it.

Society tends to discount the way boys are feeling. They may show their feelings and we ignore them. We assume they're going to get better on their own because they don't have as many emotions. Men may not understand women, but we also haven't taken the time to understand that men actually have feelings.

Women can't expect to see change from men without being willing to address some of our own beliefs and biases about emotions, and who is entitled to show them. There are several women who buy into the whole "emotions make men less manly" way of thinking.

Recently, I've been trying to talk to my guy friends more about feelings and emotions, even if it's to let them know having a good cry every once in a while is super helpful. I ask a lot of them if they've ever cried, and most of them say they don't, or never have. If a guy friend ever says something like this, I encourage you to tell them it's okay to cry, or to let their feelings out. If they hear it enough, maybe it'll change the way they think.

Men are more afraid to cry in front of other men than they are women. But I still like to believe that if they hear it enough from women their thoughts surrounding showing their emotions will start to change.

My dad has always been really comfortable with showing his emotions. I've seen him cry quite a bit, and he's pretty open about when he's feeling upset. He says a million times a day how much he loves my mom, sister and me. It's super sweet, and I know how lucky I am. He and my mom always made sure to make us feel like our emotions were valid, and if we needed to talk about stuff, they were willing to listen. I feel lucky having a dad who wanted to hear about the things that were bothering me, and I never felt uncomfortable talking to him about anything and everything.

My friends always comment on my relationship with my parents, and how close we are as a family. We talk to each other about literally everything, and there's nothing I could say that would make my parents judge me. And I've done some pretty questionable shit in my lifetime. Growing up in a judgement-free and very understanding household was pretty great. Opening the lines of communication between you and the people you love and care about is really important. I knew my parents weren't going to get angry or think less of me for what I was doing. They didn't let me get away with murder, though! If I did something wrong or stupid, we talked about it, but in a really constructive way. In my house, emotions were a completely normal thing.

I never thought of having emotions as a bad thing within my immediate household, because I wasn't taught they were (the outside world is a different story). Both of my parents are sensitive, caring people who listened to our happiness, anger and sadness. I'm not perfect and neither are my parents. Certain things that worked for my family might not work for others, and that's fine. I believe people really benefit from having more communication. We need to encourage people to have an emotional outlet or someone they can talk to. Whether it's family, friends or a professional.

This kind of growth starts from a young age. We need to stop admonishing boys for crying, and instead ask them why they're feeling this way, and give them tools to address their feelings. If we begin to do things like this it will shape our world differently.

We force people to be afraid of their own feelings rather than embracing them. It has nothing to do with being a man or being strong. Telling people not to show emotions is like telling people not to breathe. It's ridiculous to pretend they don't exist.

I've talked a lot about how we've failed women throughout this book, but teaching people to hide their emotions has hurt both men and women. Men don't know how to address their own emotions, and even having them is scary for some. Not allowing men to have an emotional outlet is unfair. It's also led to some men having a negative perception of women because we are emotional. They naturally assume we're weak because of it. I challenge these men to think differently. Maybe showing emotions makes us strong.

Vulnerability is a scary thing, and it's something I've struggled with my whole life. I've been working on allowing people to see that vulnerable side of me, but it's not always easy with men. I worry they'll judge me for having a lot of emotions, or they won't understand where I'm coming from. Fully allowing people to see you as you are can be terrifying, but it doesn't have to be. The reason why it's terrifying is because we've made it that way.

I always thought of myself as a pretty vulnerable person, but I was wrong. When I went to university and became immersed in a more serious environment, I found I began to have more fear about showing my emotions. Going into a male-dominated field made me guarded. I no longer felt comfortable to be my once emotional self. I didn't want to appear as weak. I knew that once I left university and entered the working world, there would be no place for emotions, so I forced myself to tone it down a little bit. I had someone very close call me out on it one time. She noticed I was struggling emotionally, and she said to me "You aren't in business school anymore, Janine. Stop hiding and let people in." I never realized it, but she was so right. Not letting people in was affecting my personal life. And as soon as she called me out on it, I started to break down the walls I had been building up over the last seven years.

Thinking about how difficult it was and is, for me to be vulnerable, put into perspective how difficult it must be for men to be vulnerable. If I'm this scared to do it, I know they are probably just as scared. If I had built these walls up, surely they've done the same. The fear I felt in being vulnerable around men, they are feeling that exact same fear, but probably ten times the amount I am. I know that many men are unwilling to let someone in, not out of stubbornness, but out of fear. Thinking that who you are isn't enough for some people is a really scary thing to accept. Who are we to deny someone the right to feeling vulnerable? Who are we to make someone feel scared about doing something so human? I will never judge men for being vulnerable. I will never think any less of them for being this way. They are deserving of love and respect at all times. Not just when they are being society's definition of strong.

It's so frustrating when someone tells you not to feel sad. We can't tell people to just "man up" and then show almost no compassion towards that person. I would not handle that well, personally. It would make me feel so much worse! That type of response has got to have a negative effect on everyone, not just me. It's so ridiculous that someone can think that telling someone to hide their emotions makes those emotions go away. THEY ARE STILL THERE! They are still affecting that person. I feel the need to really drive that point home. What a dumb thing to say to someone, honestly. It's such a fucking lazy solution. We have seen a ton of evidence showing why that's not okay, and the harm it can inflict on someone. It causes men to be emotionally immature and emotionally stunted. While some people are moving away from these beliefs, there are still so many people who reject this evidence and continue to treat men like they don't feel pain. Learn from the past, people. Especially when the evidence is staring you in the face.

Not allowing men to show their emotions hurts people in many different ways. More ways, I think, than people realize. Making people feel stupid or bad for showing their feelings is one of the worst things someone can do. We've been teaching boys that showing their emotions is stupid, so that's how they react when we show them ours. It's all some of them know.

We've also taught men that, for the most part, there is only one way for them to show emotions—anger. I find it really interesting that society has deemed this okay because when I see someone absolutely losing their shit I don't think, "Wow, that guy is really strong." If anything, I think the opposite. Anger is not an appropriate way to exhibit your emotions all the time. It's actually really unhealthy. If all someone knows is anger, it will cause them to deal with their emotions in the wrong way, and there will be no release.

Some men think jumping right to anger is an appropriate way to deal with a situation when, in some cases, it really doesn't solve anything. It turns people off, and prevents you from getting to the root of the problem. If someone's yelling at me, I'm not going to feel comfortable talking to them about anything. It creates more problems rather than fixing them.

It's time we changed the conversation surrounding emotions. Everyone needs to make a concerted effort towards these changes. We all have played a part, to some extent, in creating a world that shames men for showing their emotions. If you aren't part of the solution, you're part of the problem. Emotions don't have to be something we run from. This world can be difficult enough without people feeling the need to hide behind a mask.

# 22

# My Bachelor-Watching Origin Story

*"Macho does not prove mucho"*
– ZsaZsa Gabor

My friend from university, Cam, and I moved to Toronto within a month of each other. We had always been friends in university, but once we both moved to the same new city we started spending more time together one-on-one. It was nice to have someone who was familiar and from back home. We didn't see each other that often. Maybe a couple times a month, if that. We were hanging out one day and he said to me, "Do you watch The Bachelor?"

"No," I replied. "I've never seen it. Not really my thing."

"Okay, well, that needs to change, because I need someone to watch it with." He went on to tell me how he and his guy friends used to get together and watch it all the time, and it just wouldn't be the same watching it by himself. He loves the show.

"It starts next Monday. I'll bring the rosé." According to Cam, every Bachelor night needs a bottle of rosé. So there we were, two friends, eating snacks, and enjoying The Bachelor together with a glass of rosé in hand every Monday night.

Cam is a straight man.

Cam was the captain of our university football team.

Cam unapologetically loves The Bachelor.

Not only did we watch it, but we would talk about what was happening as the episode unfolded. I found out nothing bothered

Cam more than when they picked out outfits he thought were wrong for the occasion. Or outfits he didn't think were that nice.

"I think I should be a stylist for The Bachelor. I'd do a lot better job than these people," he proudly declared.

He then told me, "If you ever go on this show, you're hiring me to be your stylist. I would never let them do you dirty like that." It was very nice of him to assume people would want to watch me on that show. He has a lot of faith in how interesting I am, I guess.

Watching The Bachelor brought Cam and I closer than ever. We went from seeing each other a couple of times a month to a couple of times a week. He's been there for me when I needed him, and I was never afraid to be vulnerable in front of him. Cam has allowed me to express all my feelings and emotions to him, and he always manages to give advice while putting a smile on my face. Once his girlfriend, Sarah, moved to Toronto the three of us became like a little family. I could depend on those two for anything. And I became a third wheel they'll never be able to get rid of.

It's crazy to think a reality TV show got us to this point. It might never have happened if Cam had been too worried about his masculinity to watch the show and admit how much he loved it.

Men like Cam are important. They set an example for other men about how it's okay to enjoy things not considered "manly." Cam is Cam. The fact that he likes The Bachelor doesn't change the way I think about him in any way. If anything, it made me respect him even more.

It may seem small, but this type of attitude from men can inspire big changes. It gives men permission to like whatever the hell they want to like and not be embarrassed by it. Knowing they aren't going to be judged by the people around them for liking something shows people they can be their true selves. It also tells people the things women are interested in aren't trivial or stupid. And it allows men and women to spend time together doing something that brings both of them enjoyment.

# 23
# The Double Standards

*"Success has made failures of many men."*
*– Cindy Adams*

Sometimes men will use their emotions only when it will directly benefit them. They put on a show because they think showing their emotional side will get them out of trouble. This is very common when powerful men find themselves in hot water. They've done something awful and they are seen as monsters. They think showing their emotions will restore some of their humanity in the eye of the public. And they're right. A lot of the time it works for them . . . as long as they're white.

We see white men accused of sexual assault, and when they're addressing their actions, whether it be to the court or public, they're emotional. They plead for leniency by saying thirty minutes of misjudgment shouldn't ruin the rest of their lives. They won't do it again, and they made a mistake. And don't worry! They promise they're good guys, and maybe their accuser is just confused about what happened. They're showing us this must be true because, look! They're crying. They must mean what they say. We fall for it so fucking easily.

Many times these white men are acquitted or serve very little jail time. Part of it is because there are people who genuinely believe them, and don't think their lives should be ruined because of one mistake. The other part is we've built a system that always puts white male lives first. The public believes their show of emotions because they've talked themselves into believing it's true due to their inherent biases.

But what about the woman in this scenario? She's also showing her emotions and saying she didn't deserve what happened to her. She's telling us those thirty minutes have ruined her life, and she is demanding justice. But it doesn't matter what she says, because she's already lost. We have become so desensitized to women's emotions that we don't care when they show them. No matter the scenario. Some people will say this girl is being too emotional, and that what he did to her isn't worth ruining his life. Other people will say she's playing it up, and they don't believe her. Why is he allowed to show emotions, but she isn't? Why are his emotions valid, and not hers?

This is just another way in which society has failed women. It's told us we're too emotional, and we show our feelings at inappropriate times, therefore we can't be taken seriously. Yet when we are showing our emotions in a situation that's deemed appropriate, they still don't take us seriously. There is no scenario in which women can win.

Sometimes we'll see a man get emotional when they're in legal trouble, and the woman who accuses them is the picture of stoic. She's poised and professional and not showing a shred of emotion. She knows if she does, she won't be taken seriously. The man in this situation is allowed to show his emotions, but she isn't. She needs to work way harder than him in order to be taken seriously. The double standard is so obvious it hurts. But we've blinded ourselves to these injustices, we don't even realize we're doing it. We don't take women seriously, and we take a man's word over a woman's.

I remember watching Christine Blasey Ford's testimony about her sexual assault by Brett Kavanaugh. Brett Kavanaugh is a judge on the Supreme Court in the USA. Throughout her testimony, Christine was poised and strong. She didn't shed a single tear, and she really didn't get overly worked up. Brett Kavanaugh was a different story. He was extremely emotional. I don't think it was a surprise to anyone that Kavanaugh was allowed to keep his position on the Supreme Court.

Imagine if in this same situation she had been emotional, and he hadn't. People would have been so quick to dismiss her. They would have taken her less seriously than they already did. If she had shown the same level of emotion as Kavanaugh did, she would have been torn apart by the media and society. She was torn down the minute she opened up about her experience with him. It would have been worse for her if she had been emotional. I admire her strength and her poise. I wouldn't have been able to stand up there the way she did and maintain the type of composure she was capable of. She probably knew she had to keep herself composed because anything less would have caused her to lose what little credibility she already had. This woman stood up in front of the whole world and put herself in a very vulnerable position. We don't take the words of women seriously. Or we make excuses for the shitty way men treat women.

The bottom line is, women shouldn't have to work this hard to be taken seriously. Our truth shouldn't get pushed aside the second it's up against a white man's. We also shouldn't have to continuously fight our own emotions just for people to take what we say seriously. And we definitely shouldn't have to fight them because we're scared someone might think we're crazy.

A powerful man is only as powerful as his image. When that image is torn down, he will do everything he can in order to build it back up in people's minds. It's interesting how we judge emotions so strongly, yet showing emotions is the first way these men try to repair that image. When everything is said and done, we want to see other people's humanity. Yet somehow, we are always trying to fight this.

The men who crucify people for showing their emotions, but then turn around and use their own emotions to their benefit, are terrible people. Either emotions are bad, or they aren't. We can't allow only some people to get away with showing them. It's all or nothing.

There's also a double standard when we view women as crazy and not men. "All women are crazy" is a very normal thing for people, especially men, to say. They think we're crazy and psychotic and that's the stereotype we've been given. Men do some of the craziest shit in this world, and nobody ever thinks of them this way. I don't know one man who is afraid of being killed for rejecting a woman, but I know several women who are scared to turn a man down. The things men do to women are bat shit fucking crazy sometimes, yet they've never been labeled this way.

The behaviour women exhibit isn't any crazier than the behaviour men exhibit. It's just different behaviour. They may react to situations differently. Both are capable of doing some fucked up stuff. The only difference is we fault one gender for it and not the other.

Even if women were to start saying "all men are crazy," it would never stick. This world has a history of not taking what women say seriously. We could never give men a label like this because they would decide they didn't want it, and it wouldn't happen. Calling women psychotic is just another way society uses to put women down.

Women being called "bitchy" or "bossy" when they are being confident is another emotional double standard we have to deal with. Men can exhibit this behaviour all they want, and people praise them. When women do it, we get the opposite. Some men have actually found a way to make us incompetent no matter what emotion we are showing.

The double standard of women being allowed to cry but not men could be used as an argument against what I've just said. However, there are two problems with this thought. The first is, men created that issue, not women. That double standard exists because of men's fragile masculinity. The second is, when men cry, they are viewed as being too womanly, something that no man should want to be. Women still end up on the losing end of that double standard.

There are so many double standards between men and women which are prevalent in society. They're so harmful to women and the way in which we think about women. It's time to stop faulting women for things men don't have to worry about.

# 24
# Men Leading By Example

*"A feminist is anyone who recognizes the equality and full humanity of women and men."*
– Gloria Steinam

While it's important for everyone to do their part in changing the conversation surrounding emotions, men have the opportunity to make the most impact. If men see other men owning their own and others' emotions, it will start to become more widely accepted. If men start to teach their children that emotions are a healthy thing, they will grow up believing that to be true. Change won't happen overnight, but taking steps right away will have immediate and lasting effects.

I genuinely don't know anyone who looks at a man who won't show emotion and thinks, "Oh yeah, that's one emotionally stable person." Including other men! As much as I'm sick of men not showing emotions, I imagine most of them are just as sick of it. Eventually that shit really starts to weigh on a person. So let's just say "fuck it" to everything we've been believing and doing up until this point.

The challenge is getting men to also say "fuck it." It's really not easy to reverse literal centuries of telling men that to be tough means to not talk about or show your feelings. We've got to shatter the stereotypes surrounding both men and women.

For men, it's all about learning and being open to hearing some harsh truths. By having these conversations, they may come to understand they have these sexist beliefs without even realizing they had them in the first place. They may also realize they've done some sexist things in the past. As long as they're making a conscious effort to change these beliefs, we can't fault them. It's going to take a lot of learning and trying, and there are times they're going to fail. If they do, that's fine. Getting angry when, or if, they fail will benefit no one. All it takes is a gentle reminder to get them back on track. I know several men who are really good at listening, and when I've had conversations with them about how difficult it is to be a woman they take everything in. They ask questions, and it's obvious they're trying to learn.

Men look to other men for guidance. It would honestly be so great if a guy could say to his buddies, "Nah, I can't come out tonight, I have my sewing class," without feeling judged. Women do "male" activities all the time without the judgement of other women. I'll watch football, or go fishing, and my female friends don't even bat an eye. They don't think it's going to make me any less of a woman, because women don't care about shit like that. I really would love to walk into a nail salon and see all these guy friends getting their nails done together. It's not weird. The only reason it's weird is because we've made it that way. So let's just unmake it that way. You want to carry a purse, then go ahead and carry a fucking purse. Not allowing men to do things because it might make them seem more female is insulting to women. You think our gender is so bad you're going to ridicule other men for displaying these qualities? Fuck off with that bullshit. Let them be who they want to be.

Men, stop thinking of certain things as "female." It's really fucking silly. Just live your life the way you want to live it. Being scared to do things because people won't think you're manly is, ironically, not very manly—if you follow that way of thinking. Men want to be these tough, fearless dudes, but are scared to be themselves. They run from their feelings rather than address them. That's like the opposite of fearless. Men, unfortunately, don't see it the same way though.

Manliness comes in all different shapes and sizes. There is no clear-cut definition of manliness. If you're a man, then you're a man, and nothing you do can take away from that fact. And don't let anyone take that away from you. People are going to judge no matter what, and living your life to try and please others is an already lost battle. The most important person you should be trying to please is yourself. Being yourself and honouring your needs, wants and emotions are essential. In my opinion, if this is the way you're living your life, then you are about as fucking manly as you can get.

The dads of this world are the best examples their boys can have. If they see their dad treating women with respect, chances are they're going to grow up also treating women with respect. Dads need to talk to their sons about their emotions. Don't tell them they can't show them. A dad admonishing his son for showing emotions is traumatizing. Hearing that come from one of the people they love most in the world will scare them into never doing it again. It's so important to be there for your child. Let them know what they're feeling is valid, and that you're there to help them through it. If they can do this from a young age, their emotional health as an adult will be much stronger. It's not enough to see one of your parents doing it either. Both need to make a conscious effort in shaping the way young children feel about their emotions and showing them.

Representation in the media would also be beneficial for men. Seeing films surrounding men's emotions, and seeing men cry would give other men permission to do the same thing. Making this a less taboo topic, and creating regular content about men's feelings would in turn make men feel less weird about their emotions. Drawing more attention to male celebrities or people of influence who embrace their emotions can also help men see that this is normal behaviour. Celebrities have a ton of influence on people, but especially young people.

For all the women reading this book, I assume you and your female friends compliment each other all the time. We're always telling each other we're beautiful or that we like each other's outfits or hair. We compliment each other non-stop. When's the last time you heard a man say to another man, "I like that haircut on you. You look handsome"? My guess would be never. Because I certainly haven't. Telling your guy friends they look good doesn't make you any less of a man. You, as a man, are allowed to think other men are attractive.

Also, for the love of god, please make it normal for men to cry in front of their male friends. Everyone needs an outlet, and denying yourself an outlet isn't helping anyone. We surround ourselves with people we trust for support. If you aren't able to comfortably open up to these people, you might need to re-evaluate your friend choices. Mental health is not something to dick around with, and so many men struggle with their mental health. They don't have the same types of support systems women have, and they're used to shoving their emotions deep down inside themselves. All men feel things, so men need to stop pretending they don't. Men need other men for support. Coming to women is all well and good, but having someone who understands what you're going through is much more beneficial. There are some things—with regard to men—that no matter what, women can't relate to, and vice versa.

Fear of being judged is really scary for people. I'm scared of being judged, I'm not going to pretend I'm not. Men fear this judgement mostly from other men. They think being manly is the most important thing you can be, and it's affected how they live their lives. But society is starting to say otherwise. We've got a long way to go, but men showing their emotions is much accepted now then it was before.

I also know a lot of women who are immediately turned off when they find out a guy is that manly man type who won't show any sort of emotion. Most of us don't want that. It's always such a huge relief to me when I date a guy who is emotional, and won't laugh at me for showing my feelings, too. So, if nothing else, men should show their emotions to get the ladies!

In all seriousness though, when I'm looking to date someone, I need to know they're able to show feelings. I don't feel comfortable around men who are scared of their emotions, let alone wanting to date one of them. To me, it's incredibly attractive when a man is able to express himself emotionally, because I know it allows for a deeper connection in the relationship.

Men have a responsibility toward both women and other men to do better and lead by example. Knowing there are men who think this way, and accept this responsibility is really comforting. There are a lot of men out there who are doing a great job trying to break down those stereotypes. Who aren't afraid to make it known that they are emotional. The benefits to changing our ways of thinking are endless.

# 25

# The Importance of Emotional Education

*"All of us are put in boxes by our family, by our religion, by our society, our moment in history, even our own bodies. Some people have the courage to break free."*

– Geena Rocero

A big part of society's problem is we don't teach people how to manage and work through their emotions. Instead, we've stigmatized them and turned them into a bad thing. People are so scared to address their feelings or admit that their emotional health is suffering. We are told not to show emotions, or that emotions are a weakness. That's it. That's all we're told. And when we get into a situation where we might get emotional, we focus so hard on not getting emotional it affects the way we behave in said situation. The more I try to not get emotional, the more emotional I get. It's a slippery slope. Rather than have someone teach us how to use our emotions and to work through them in a constructive manner, we've made people feel bad for having them. This doesn't benefit anyone.

We need to teach children about their emotions and how important it is to have a support system. The more we stigmatize them, the less likely people will search for ways to better their emotional health. We need to encourage adults to address their emotions as well, and to help others become more comfortable around people who show them.

I grew up always putting other people's feelings before mine. If someone wanted to do something I didn't want to do, I would do it anyways to make them happy. I avoided confrontation like the fucking plague because I thought telling someone they hurt me would make them feel bad about themselves. So even though people have done some really horrible things to me, I would never bring it up because I didn't want them to feel bad. What a dumb way of thinking. I've grown a lot throughout my life, but this is something I'm always going to struggle with.

I recently met up with a friend of mine who I haven't seen in a few years. When I moved to Toronto from Winnipeg the big city changed me, apparently. I was telling him a story about how I really had to stand up for myself and made a big confrontation to someone. He was blown away that I was able to do this, and told me I never would have done something like this three years ago living in Winnipeg. I was thinking to myself, *Oh fuck yeah. Does this make me super tough?* It doesn't, but still. I was able to stand up to this person. Did I hold my ground? Yes. Did I cry the second she walked away from me? Of course I did. It sucked, and I hated every second of it, but it had to be done.

It's crazy that it took so many years for me to do something like this though. The person I had to stand up to was walking all over me and taking advantage of me like you wouldn't believe. I know I should have stood up to her a lot sooner. Baby steps, okay?

We need to teach people, especially women, that it's okay to tell people when they're hurting you. Women are constantly putting other people's feelings ahead of their own. I know I have a lot of work to do still, but little victories are something to be celebrated.

It's so important to teach men that having emotions doesn't make you weak or any less capable of success. Some men disregard women's abilities because they don't have the knowledge to understand that emotions are not a flaw.

We have to give people the tools they need to help others when they're showing emotion. We also need to learn how to recognize when someone's emotional well-being is at risk, or if there's any concern over someone's mental health. If someone isn't behaving the way they normally would, it is completely unacceptable to judge or belittle them for it.

The more we teach men and women about emotions and all the different shapes and forms they may take, the better off everyone will be. If everyone became a little more informed or accepting about men and women's emotions, the world would be in a much better place. There is always room to listen and grow, and by doing this we would see a lot more equality.

So much can be accomplished by just listening. The more we find out about people's emotions, the more we'll learn about them. For some men, navigating an emotional landscape is unchartered territory. They haven't ever listened to anyone talking about their feelings, so they will be completely lost. Of course, someone in this situation is going to want to completely avoid it. They have no idea what to do. It sounds crazy, but they may not even know the first thing to do to help at all.

I'm not saying that everyone should consult a therapist or professional in order to learn about emotions and feelings. Sometimes the simplest solution is enough. We can find out so much by just talking to and listening to people when they speak. Sometimes being there and not saying anything is enough for some people. There is no cookie-cutter response to dealing with someone's emotions. Everyone is different. This is why it's important to be open to listening and learning new things. But when having someone be there for you isn't enough, there's no shame in recognizing the need to talk to a therapist. A therapist is just a normal person who is trained to help deal with emotions, and to suggest ways to manage your emotions when they get overwhelming. Unfortunately there is still a stigma surrounding therapists, but big strides have been made in accepting the need for therapy as normal.

Would it be such a crazy thing to suggest we start teaching these things to children in school? We put so much importance on academic learning, but there is so much more to life than this. Having a lot of academic knowledge is all well and good until life swoops in and knocks you off your feet. There needs to be more of a focus on effective communication and listening in schools. This can be done in early years education. Kids need to learn how to work through their problems on their own. They need to learn how to speak up, know when they're hurt, and know when they've hurt someone. They also need to know that seeing a therapist is totally fine. It doesn't make you crazy. If we can see a doctor about our physical health, we can see a therapist for our mental health. It's important to let kids know that there are always options out there for them when they are having difficulty handling their emotions. Putting an emphasis on emotional learning is just as important as academic learning, yet we don't address it at all.

If we were to address it at an early age, children would grow up knowing how to better handle their emotions. This would naturally lead to less divisive beliefs about men versus women.

We also need to learn that even though people's emotions are valid, the way we act on those emotions may not be. If something makes you angry, it's fine to feel angry. But if you take that anger out on someone else, you'd be acting like an asshole. I'm guilty of doing this. I've taken my emotions out on the people I care about. I've been that asshole before. I think we all have. So while it's important to recognize your emotions as valid, and not be upset with yourself when you feel things, it's just as important to respond appropriately to those emotions. Everyone has their own strategy when it comes to processing their emotions. For some it's breathing, others it's counting. There's no right or wrong way to process how you're feeling. Giving people an emotional education, especially at a young age, will allow people to recognize how they best respond to their own emotions and discover strategies to cope with them.

If we allowed everyone to show their emotions freely, we also might begin to understand each other on a deeper level. If we took it a step further and tried to learn about someone's feelings and how it's affecting them, it might lead to more empathetic responses from others. Knowing how emotions affect other people will lead us to be more forgiving of things we previously didn't understand. Think of what might happen if the world had more understanding and empathy. I see some pretty big changes that can only lead to good things.

## 26
# Little Emotions

*"Little girls with dreams become women with a vision."*
*– Unknown*

I teach English to kids in China. It's all done one-on-one over the internet, but I've made some pretty strong connections with some of my students. I have this little five year old who is quite possibly the smartest person I've ever met. She's smarter than I am, that's for sure, and I make sure to tell her that all the time. And I know we aren't supposed to have favourites, but this kid is definitely my favourite. I love this kid, and she loves me. It's pretty cute.

One day she came to class and she looked really sad. I could see it all over her sweet little face.

"Are you okay?" I asked her.

She couldn't say anything. She just started crying really hard, and she wouldn't look at me. It seemed she was a little embarrassed about her crying. I told her that her feelings were valid and whatever she was feeling was okay.

"Take a minute and cry it out. If you want to tell me why you're upset you can, and if you don't, that's okay too," I explained to her.

She silently cried for about a minute, and then in her small voice she looked at me and said, "I want to talk about it."

So we spent a little bit of time talking about why she was upset. I told her that what happened would have made me sad too. I validated her feelings and made sure I was there for her as best as I could be over a computer screen. What I really wanted to drive into her was everything she was feeling was okay, and that talking about it was a good way to process emotions. I also told her I wished I could be there to give her a big squeeze. I ended up making her laugh and she was very quickly back to her usual smiling self.

A couple months later I lost someone very important to me. I teach these kids really early in the morning, and I didn't sleep at all the night before. I had spent most of the night crying. I looked like hell in the morning. When I saw this girl for our class, she looked at me for a little bit and said, "Your eyes look sad." I'm telling you, this kid is a little genius.

"I'm feeling a little sad today," I told her while trying to put a genuine smile on my face.

"It's okay to feel sad. You can be sad," she explained to me very gently. "Remember when I was sad, and you said it was okay?"

So she and I talked about why I was sad. She was there for me because I was there for her, and she now knows that the emotions we feel are valid. My heart was ready to burst. It might be the sweetest thing that's ever happened to me.

"I wish I could be there to give you a big squeeze," she said, using the words she and I so often say to one another.

She made me feel a lot better. It just goes to show you don't need to do a lot to be there for someone. Sometimes all it takes is something really small. Maybe it'll make someone feel better, and maybe it won't. At least they know you're willing to be there for them.

Teaching kids it's okay to feel their feelings is so important. My student recognized that something about me was a little off, and she questioned me about it. Despite my brave face, this five year old was able to tell something was wrong with me. If she was able to recognize it and help me through it, adults can do the same thing for one another. She made me feel a lot better, and we had a two-minute conversation about it. When she was sad, her and I were still able to complete our lesson effectively. When I was sad it was the same outcome.

The point is, both of us were able to continue on with our lives. We were still able to be productive, but we knew about each other's feelings. Whether someone is big or small, they are capable of talking about emotions in an effective manner.

## 27

# On Being a Drama Queen

*"If you don't like the road you're walking,
start paving another one."*
– Dolly Parton

If you were to ask my friends and family to describe me, they would probably all say that I'm a pretty dramatic and emotional person. And I would say they're right. I am super emotional. Normally, being a drama queen is thought of as a negative. Out of curiosity, I looked up "being a drama queen" on Google, and one of the first things to pop up is an article on how to stop being a drama queen. I also found advice on how to deal with a drama queen, and why it's bad to be one. Very rude of those articles to assume I want to stop being a drama queen, or that I'm hard to deal with! If you were to ask my friends if I was difficult to deal with, none of them would say I am. Or maybe they're a bunch of cowards who would say I was behind my back. Kidding. My friends are great and supportive.

I know that I'm a feeler. When I'm happy, I'm really happy, and when I'm sad, I get really sad. There's nothing wrong with that; it just means that I get affected by events that happen in my life. The way I react to those events is normal, despite what society might tell me. I know there are times in my life when I am over-dramatic about something that happens, but who isn't? When I say something like "I'm so thirsty, I'd punch someone in the throat for a glass of water," I don't actually mean that. I'm definitely being dramatic when I say stuff like this, but I'm also just kind of being an idiot.

But I started thinking, maybe I'm not actually a drama queen. Maybe everything I thought about myself up to this point was wrong. Just because I'm in tune with my emotions, and I can express the way I'm feeling doesn't necessarily mean I'm being dramatic. It just means I'm being a human. We assume that when we encounter an emotional woman, she's being a drama queen, when she's actually just feeling her emotions. We have this warped view of women, and we assume they're being crazy and over the top whenever they exhibit any sort of feeling.

Even if I am a drama queen though, there's nothing wrong with it. Being a drama queen means reacting to things in a dramatic way. But who gets to decide what a dramatic response is? A response is a response. Just because someone wouldn't respond with the type of feeling someone else would doesn't mean their way of responding is the only right way. People are so judgmental about other people. Let people live their lives, and if you don't like the way someone does something, deal with it.

I don't get offended when people tell me I'm dramatic. I call myself dramatic all the time. It's something I can laugh at about myself, and I like to not take myself too seriously. But being emotional doesn't automatically equal dramatic. People feel what they feel, and we're all going to express those feelings differently.

I knew a girl who used to cry over everything. Like literally everything, I'm not exaggerating. Everyone always used to call this girl a drama queen, and she was made fun of for it constantly. Could you imagine being laughed at over your emotions? I bet this poor girl felt really shitty every time she cried. She wasn't "being a drama queen" though. She was just feeling her feelings, and no matter what she did, she was going to cry, whatever the situation. She wasn't trying to get attention, or pity, or whatever it is people assume women are trying to get when they cry. She was emotional, and she couldn't control that. I don't think she should have had to control it either. I bet she would have given anything to be able to hold back her tears. Nobody wants to be made fun of like that.

I also remember having so much second-hand embarrassment for this girl. Every time she cried, I would think, *Oh god, why does she do that?* It was a really awful way for me to think. Even though I wouldn't make fun of her directly, my thoughts about her feelings were just as harmful to her. She didn't deserve any sort of judgement from anyone, especially not me, because she was a friend of mine. Imagine how much better she would have felt if I had sat with her when she cried, or tried to talk about it. She probably felt so alone and embarrassed, which probably led to her feeling more emotional. What a roller coaster for this poor girl.

I'm also unaware of any words we might use to describe an overly emotional man. Have you ever seen a guy freak the fuck out over the results of a sporting event? If the game means a lot to him and he's upset over the outcome that's totally fine. His feelings are valid. But if a woman were to cry and yell over the results of a game, we would tell her she was being overly emotional.

Watch some men play golf or tennis and you'll see them throw their clubs in the water or snap their racquet. I've never seen a woman do this in golf or tennis. I'm sure it happens, but not to the degree it happens with men. This type of behaviour is the definition of dramatic. But nobody will say this to men, or think of men as being this way. It's because men have controlled the narrative over women's behaviour for way too long. Some men want women to be seen as lesser, so they attack women for certain behaviours, but allow themselves to get away with doing the very same thing.

The Vancouver Canucks lost the Stanley Cup playoffs in 2011, and the fans started a full-blown riot. Because a large number of the fans were male, it can be assumed a large percentage of the rioters were men. I mean, that's a pretty fucking emotional response to a team losing. Their actions were condemned, yes, but stuff like that doesn't define men. When we see them doing stuff like that, we don't call them drama queens.

Men can get away with things women can't. Think about the roles being reversed, and the women starting a riot over something viewed as more female. Like the results of the Bachelor. It sounds insane because people will say, "Who would start a riot over The Bachelor?" But I would also like to ask, "Who would start a riot over a hockey game?" Seriously, think about it for a second. If women were to do this, we would never live it down. People would use it as an excuse for women's incapability forever. We could never get away with something like this.

Women start riots over things like gender inequality, and the wage gap, and we're met with judgement over it. We're told these things don't exist, and we're blowing it out of proportion. Despite there being mountains of evidence, people don't believe there's an issue. We're thought of as drama queens when we riot over things like human rights, and we're just "being emotional." So, a riot over a sporting event can be overlooked, but not something like gender inequality. It doesn't make any sense. The results of a sporting event are not equal to a human rights issue. Women are not exclusively drama queens.

We need to stop giving women all these negative labels. They do nothing but harm. Think about all the things people have told you about your emotions. Think about how many of those things were negative. We are so judgemental about everything women do. Using words like "drama queen" makes society think women are difficult to deal with, when they aren't.

For now, I'm going to continue loving when people call me a drama queen. I know it's all for fun, and I think of it as part of what makes me so great. People aren't saying this to me in order to be malicious. Nobody actually thinks I'm difficult. And if they do, they can fuck off. Showing my emotions doesn't make me, or anyone else difficult. It makes us human.

# 28
# Say Goodbye to Proper

*"Life is not measured by the number of breaths we take, but by the moments that take our breath away"*

*– Maya Angelou*

On June 2, 2019, I sat in the small room of my Grandma's nursing home waiting for her to die. She was ninety-eight years old and a fighter to the end. My Grandma was a hell of a woman. She was strong, smart, beautiful, and had the kindest heart you would ever meet. I sit here writing about her with the biggest smile on my face, remembering this remarkable woman.

Everyone was gathered together in her room to say our goodbyes and to be with her in her final moments. A palpable sadness lingered in the room. Silence filled the tiny room except for the odd sniffle. My grandma lay in her bed unable to recognize us, but hopefully able to hear. I'd like to think she was able to hear what was going on around her. That she would have known there were so many people who loved her who were there to say goodbye.

She meant so much to so many people, and living without her was something we were all trying to learn to accept in a short amount of time. Living without her was something we all knew would happen eventually, but still hated that it had to happen.

As the room filled with my large family the space got smaller, and the room was getting increasingly warm. My mom, bless her heart, started to take off her sweater and with the poorest choice of words said, "Is anyone else dying in here?"

"Yeah. Mom," one of my smartass uncles replied.

In a single moment all the somber feelings in the room disappeared, and instead it was filled with laughter. Now when the tears fell, they were accompanied by giggles. This is what my Grandma would have wanted. She would have appreciated the joke at her expense, and she would have joined in with us. We knew she would have felt this way, so it made it even funnier. We started telling stories about her, and even more laughs found their way into the room. I find it comforting that some of her final moments were filled with her family's laughter, a sound she had heard consistently throughout her long life.

There is no right way to show feelings. A moment of sadness can be felt with something other than tears. There might be someone out there horrified at the joke my uncle made. They might think it was not a proper time to say such a thing. But to that I would say my Grandma got to spend one last time with her family hearing them laugh, rather than hearing them cry. I hope it gave her peace, because it gave me some. I know it's what she would have wanted, and I will always remember that moment. A little bit of sunshine on what was a pretty gray day.

There is no "proper" form of expression when it comes to your emotions. They will manifest themselves in ways that may be unexpected. It doesn't mean they're wrong. Your feelings are never wrong. Don't be proper, because proper is boring. Proper is limiting. Proper takes the laughter out of a dying woman's room.

# 29

# Owning Your Emotions

*"You may encounter many defeats, but you must not be defeated. In fact, it may be necessary to encounter the defeats, so you can know who you are, what you can rise from, how you can still come out of it."*

– *Maya Angelou*

There are always going to be people who have a problem with emotions, and who think they're a sign of weakness. There are always going to be judgemental people in the world, period. Accepting your emotions is really important for your emotional health and well-being. Fuck anyone who tells you you're too emotional. They've just decided what emotions they're okay with dealing with, and yours didn't make the cut.

I am really uninterested in living in a world that condemns people for being happy, or sad, or angry, or for showing their feelings in general. These are the things that give people character. We need to start recognizing that people aren't a bunch of robots, incapable of feeling. There's no harm in recognizing that people will get emotional all the time, in a wide range of situations. It's not up to anyone to decide when and where these emotions are allowed, or how people are allowed to show them. We all need to work a little harder in accepting vulnerability. The first step is recognizing and accepting your own vulnerability. Own that shit.

As I've gotten older, I've become way more emotional. I will cry at anything and everything. Watching movies is a nightmare because I get so worked up over every little thing that happens on screen. If I'm this way now, what am I going to be like in thirty years from now? I'm going to be a wreck. I actually kind of love this side of me, though. It tells me I'm empathetic, and I'm affected by the way other people are feeling. In no way am I ashamed of the fact that I'm getting more emotional. Bring it on.

I had a friend over once and I was going through a rough time. She came over just to talk to me about what I was dealing with and I ended up crying. She cried because she was having a hard time seeing me in pain. We somehow started talking about how much we meant to each other, and we each talked about the things we loved about the other person. It was a really meaningful moment, and I will never forget the words she said to me. I'll carry them with me forever. What she said to me was beautiful, and her crying for me was also beautiful. Our being vulnerable and emotional with one another led to some really great things. What she said to me that day meant more to me than I think she realizes, and it helped me cope with what I was going through.

It's also important to own your emotions when they come up, rather than beat yourself up for it. If they come up at what you feel is an inappropriate time, that's okay. You may have felt embarrassed after receiving negative feedback and felt like crying, or felt like crying when you were slightly admonished by someone. If this is the case, you should know that it's totally normal. People are emotional and that's fine.

I once had someone I really respected tell me, "Nobody will ever want to work with you because they'll get so sick and tired of you being so fucking happy all the time." Bit of a blow that was, especially coming from someone I looked up to. I realized two things after she said this to me: Number 1, that was a really dickish thing to say. And number 2, no matter what, there are always going to be people who hate who you are. This person didn't like the fact that I'm a happy person, and she lashed out. She used it in order to criticize me.

After a good cry, I understood what she said was a very stupid thing to say to someone. I didn't take what she said seriously, and I certainly wasn't going to change because of someone's bitter comments. If someone doesn't want to work with me because I'm happy all the time, that's fine. I probably wouldn't want to work with them either. It would probably be fucking miserable, wouldn't it? Imagine criticizing someone's happiness.

Even women are critical of other women's emotions. It's not exclusively a male thing. Everyone has it hammered into their heads that women showing emotion is a bad thing. Doesn't matter if that emotion is viewed as good or bad. This woman didn't actually think I was difficult because I was happy. For whatever reason she just wanted to bring me down. And what better way to bring a woman down then to attack her emotions. It's how we've been bringing women down for centuries.

It just goes to show how difficult it is for women. Nothing we do will ever be good enough, and there are always going to be critics. There's no emotion we can show that's the "right" emotion. This is why I'm going to take a stance and own my emotions. I recognize I'm an emotional person, and I also recognize this doesn't make me any less capable of being successful or liked.

I encourage you all to do the same thing. Own the fact that you are emotional, and stop trying to hide it. If someone has a problem with it, it's up to them to find a way to be comfortable. Women have been changing who they are for other people for a really long time. It's time that people start changing for women. Either society can accept the fact that women have emotions and they are allowed to show them, or they can fuck right off.

# 30

# What I've Learned

*"Strong men, men who are truly role models, don't need to put down women to make themselves feel powerful"*

*– Michelle Obama*

One night, I was walking outside by myself. It wasn't very late, but it was getting dark. There was this man coming towards me who gave me an uneasy feeling. My instinct told me to turn around and get out of there, but I thought to myself, *What if he's a good guy and I hurt his feelings by turning around? He'll obviously know he scared me.* I kept walking, and we passed each other without anything bad happening. Imagine if it did though.

I kept walking because I didn't want to hurt this man's feelings. A man I had no personal connection to. I felt threatened and I would have rather put myself in harm's way than maybe make him feel a little bad about himself. Who cares if he was offended! My feeling of uneasiness should have been enough for me to turn around, but I put this man before myself. I know a lot of women who would have reacted the exact same way I did. If someone is giving you a weird vibe, you avoid that person. We need to stop doing things because we might offend someone. Stop putting men, or other people in general, above your own well-being.

In my twenty-eight years of life I have learned a lot about what it means to be a woman. I've learned that it's pretty unfair in a lot of different respects. I have to think about things a man wouldn't have to think twice about. I've learned that it's hard, and there are a lot of challenges that come with being a woman. But I've also learned that it's pretty fucking great, and I wouldn't change it for anything.

One of the most important things I've learned is to surround yourself with men who don't think negatively about women showing their emotions. Or who don't think negatively about women in general. I have a lot of men in my life who I can talk to about anything and everything and they won't judge me for it. The men in my life also respect women. They believe in equality and are open to learning about issues that don't directly affect them.

Until recently, I didn't always surround myself with these types of people. There were men in my life who couldn't have cared any less about women or their feelings. They used women, and treated them terribly. These were men who used women for sex and acted like they weren't human beings. I was blinded by it because my naivety wanted me to believe these were good men. I needed to come to the understanding that not everyone is good, and if they aren't it's okay to recognize this and remove them from my life.

Whether these men were specifically using me or not is irrelevant. If they treat one woman this way, they have no respect for women in general. Not respecting women means not respecting their feelings or how actions might affect them. Some men don't care enough to see how a woman is affected by their actions every step of the way, until she decides she can't put up with it anymore. This is usually when these men start paying attention and assume she's being an emotional wreck. It's not because she's crazy, it's because she's dealt with the worst treatment possible and then finally realizes she deserves a little respect. She may be emotional, but she isn't being irrational. There's a difference, but some men are incapable of seeing it that way.

Almost every woman I know has been with a guy they trusted, only to realize they were using her for sex the entire time. They manipulated and lied to her for their own gross benefit without thinking of how it might affect the woman in the relationship. Women are worth so much more than just something to have sex with, and shame on any man who thinks otherwise. Cut that shit out of your life. You don't need it.

We've talked about some men being uncomfortable around powerful women. If you ever encounter someone like this, don't back down or let them walk all over you. We are done changing for the sake of men. Be your confident self, and if they don't like it that's a problem they have to address on their own. It really is amazing how fragile they are, but think they're these macho, masculine guys. If you feel threatened or uncomfortable just because someone has a vagina you are automatically a coward.

Sexist language and jokes don't belong in the workplace either. We hear it all the time and it's dismissed as locker room talk, or boys being boys. When we try to stop language like that we're told, "Don't be so sensitive it's just a joke." Yeah okay, but your jokes have played a hand in the oppression of women in the workplace, and allow that culture to continue. So forgive me for being a little sensitive about something that you, a man, will never understand. They throw these jokes around like they have any idea of the impact they've made on women. Call people out when shit like this happens. Men don't get to decide what's harmful. If women don't like it, stop it. And if these men don't understand why women don't like it, tell them to pick up a fucking book and educate themselves. Actually, tell them to pick up this book!

If a man in a professional setting ever talks down to you or cuts you off, simply tell them you weren't done and continue. I wrote this paragraph and then a few weeks later watched Kamala Harris look Mike Pence in the eyes and tell him, "I'm speaking," when he interrupted her during a Vice Presidential debate. Those two powerful words sent sparks flying through almost every woman I know. It was something we've all wanted to say at some point in our lives and we just witnessed a woman say it on TV for the whole world to hear. Holy shit.

Your voice deserves to be heard as much as the others, so make sure they're listening. Don't let anyone make you feel like you have to be quiet. It sounds like it might be really scary to speak up, and it can be. The first time I demanded to be heard I was terrified about what people might think. Now, I couldn't give a fuck about what people think about me.

I'm also one of those women that are constantly saying "sorry," even for doing things that I have nothing to be sorry about. There are so many women out there who are apologizers. We say sorry for absolutely everything, and we're always apologizing to men. Society has us conditioned to be this way. It's like everything we do is inconvenient for men, and whatever happens it must be our fault in some way. Stop fucking apologizing! Ladies, we are not an inconvenience, and taking ownership for someone else's mistakes allows them to avoid accountability for their actions. We have let men get away with so much because we are so quick to apologize for them. If you don't feel sorry for something, then don't say sorry. And especially don't say sorry for something that wasn't your fault. Honour your feelings, and think about whether or not you should be apologizing before doing it. Especially to men.

When we do things like this, we allow men to have a certain degree of control over our feelings. They know we're empathetic, and they'll use it to their advantage. Once it was brought to my attention how often women apologize, I noticed I was doing it all the time. That knowledge was enough for me to stop saying sorry as much. I also started to notice how much my friends would do it in front of other men as well. I brought it to their attention in the hopes they stop saying it as much. If you're like me, which I assume you are because women have always had to apologize for others, try to bring your attention to how much you're saying it.

If you're ever in that position, try just not saying it and see what happens. Not saying sorry might feel uncomfortable for you, and you may feel weird about it, but I can promise you the world isn't going to fall apart.

I've learned a lot about emotions, and I can always learn more. One of the most valuable things was learning when people are upset you don't always have to try to fix them, or make them feel better. Sometimes that person just needs you to be there for them. Maybe they even need you to be sad or upset with them. When we validate people's emotions, they are able to portray them in a healthy way. They will express them rather than keep them inside, something which has never benefited anyone. Fearing their emotions, or worse, someone's reactions to their emotions, is harmful to that individual. I've had people make me feel stupid for being upset about something, and it fucking sucks. When people do that to me it only makes me feel more distant from that person. You don't have time for my feelings, I don't have time for you. It's really that simple.

People also don't always need advice. When someone is sad and you're giving them all this harsh advice, take a step back and try to see what this might be doing to that person. It's not that hard to shut up and just be with someone every once in a while.

Everyone is going to come into their emotions in their own way and at their own pace. Pushing someone to show their emotions isn't going to be helpful. What we can do is create a safe space to let people know their emotions are welcome and unjudged. How someone chooses to respond to this is completely up to that person and that person alone.

I've come to the realization that I'm always going to have to work twice as hard to be taken as seriously as a man, and even that might not be enough. But I've also learned to keep fighting for equality because it's worth it. I'm not going to lie, sometimes it fucking exhausts me. Like really exhausts me, because it blows my mind that we still have to fight for some basic equality. But then I remember how much has changed, and it makes me feel really hopeful. There are so many powerful women in this world, and if we all use our voices someone is bound to hear. I've also learned that no matter who you are, or where you come from, you are more powerful than you think you are. Never think you are too small to make an impact on this world. More importantly, don't let anyone else tell you you're too small to make an impact. Women have made leaps when it comes to equality and it's because they started fighting one day and haven't stopped.

None of this is to say that all men are bad, and that all men are incapable of showing emotion. There are several men who are very in tune with both their feelings and women's feelings. However, as a society I think we can agree that women have been faulted for their emotions, and while we have seen some growth, there is still room for big changes.

Some of the most influential people in my life are women. Hell, some of the most influential people in the world are women. Their guidance has helped shape me into the person I am today. Look at all the powerful women you see every single day. They are going through the same struggles you are going through, but it doesn't bring them down. Just by getting up and living their lives they are fighting for change.

## 31

# Yes Babe, Feel!

*"Make yourself a better person before trying to make others better."*
– *Yao Chen*

For all the women who have ever been made to feel dumb about showing emotions, you're not alone. I think everyone, both men and women, have been in that boat at some point in their lives. Emotions are a powerful and beautiful thing. They mean you're a human being who shows compassion and empathy towards others. They mean you are affected by the events in your life or the events happening around the world. None of that should elicit feelings of shame.

The people in this world who don't show emotions may be respected, but they sure as hell aren't liked. And honestly, a lot of those people aren't even respected, they're feared. Nobody wants to be around an unrelatable robot of a person. They're the ones who have convinced people that women are impossible to work with because we're too emotional. In fact, they are the ones who are insufferable to be around.

Think of all the good things that have happened to you in your life. You wouldn't have felt that kind of happiness if it wasn't for emotions. On the flip side, you wouldn't have had those really low days without emotions, either. And those days can be really hard, but they can also help you grow as a person. Some of the most important lessons I've learned about myself came after a bout of sadness. Having these bad days didn't feel nice, but they also didn't kill me. And people always say, "What doesn't kill you makes you stronger."

Having these feelings adds so much to life. Without them, life would be pretty fucking boring, wouldn't it? You have to allow yourself to fully express your emotions in order to experience all the good and bad things life has to offer. Whoever decided they didn't want people to express their feelings needs to recognize that way of thinking is archaic. No one can or should be expected to live in such a way. These people shouldn't be the ones who make decisions for others, but a lot of the time they are the ones in powerful positions. We allow this thinking to continue and frankly, it's really dumb.

Unless you allow yourself to feel all emotions, both the good and the bad, you won't experience everything you can in this life. Allow yourself to feel, allow it to affect you, and learn from it. You don't deserve the bad things that happen to you in life. If you find you can't learn from the bad, that's okay too. Don't be hard on yourself.

Men showing their feelings doesn't make them any less of a man. Whatever the fuck that means anyways. And women showing their emotions doesn't make them a crazy lunatic. How about from now on we just stop judging people in general. You don't like the way someone's feeling? Too fucking bad, get over it. You think someone is overreacting to something? Too fucking bad, you don't know what that person is going through. This judgement may be causing us to miss out on getting to know so many great people and discovering new ideas.

Gone are the days of making people feel bad for showing their emotions. I'm over it, and you should be, too. Let's flip our way of thinking and look at it as a powerful thing. When I see someone in a position of power standing in front of everyone and showing their true emotions it's amazing. To me, there's no position you could be in that would make you more vulnerable. To be able to put yourself on display like that is one of the most powerful moves someone can make.

So many people are afraid to show their emotions because of what others might think of them. When a really monumental event happens, I want to see someone crying tears of happiness or sadness. Emotions don't make you weak, and I will say it over and over again until that starts to stick. The weak ones are the people that will judge someone for showing their emotions or think it makes them unfit for certain positions. They're the ones resistant to change even though there's so much proof that change is a good thing. We can't let these people continue to be in control and make decisions that negatively affect a large portion of the population.

It's just a fact of life that people are emotional beings. I don't know why we ever pretended otherwise. Telling people not to feel is like telling people not to eat. It's never going to happen, so why bother fighting it.

Listen to your feelings and honour them. They can lead you to a path you might never have expected yourself to be on. Ask yourself, "Am I really happy? Am I doing what's best for the life I want to live?" The more you listen to your feelings, the more you'll learn about yourself. You may discover you are capable of things you never thought yourself capable of. Be selfish. Do things for you. Change the world, or just change your world. If listening to your true feelings seems scary to you, that's because it can be terrifying. But when you try it and work past all the fear and the unknown there might be something really great waiting for you at the end of that dark tunnel. Emotions are a beautiful thing that should be celebrated, rather than something we put in a box with a pretty red bow.

Emotions are messy, frustrating, beautiful, annoying, wonderful, stupid, funny, eye-opening, and valid. You won't always like them, but you have to accept they are there and a part of life. How you act on your emotions is up to you. How you react to others' emotions is also up to you. Choose patience and understanding, with both yourself and the people around you.

I am an emotional person who didn't always love that she was emotional. I used to be embarrassed about my feelings and I used to hold them in as much as I possibly could. I've cried in a lot of bathrooms and stairwells in my life. I still don't always like that I'm an emotional person. As much as I would like to believe I am, I'm not perfect, and I'll always have room to grow. But I will say I'm more at peace with it. I'm more at peace with being who I am in general. I'm more at peace with being a woman. Life isn't fair, and I'm not going to pretend that it is. I am an emotional woman who is also very strong. I, and so many other women are living proof that it's possible to be both. We just need the rest of the world to open their eyes and see that it's possible as well. Keep being your emotional selves, ladies.

You're all powerful as hell.

# ABOUT THE AUTHOR

Janine Jeanson has observed people in a variety of settings, including the business world where she works, and has concluded that something has to change. Her passion for healing the wounds associated with strict gender roles and toxic masculinity inspired her to write *You're Probably Not Crazy*. She hopes to reach those who have been judged because of their emotions, reassure them that they're not alone, and help them find the path to healing.

Janine lives in Toronto, Ontario. *You're Probably Not Crazy* is her first book.

Printed in Canada